M000159860

DAVID MORLEY ARCHITECTS
FIVE by 5

Artifice
books on architecture

CONTENTS

F O R E W O R D

25 years of practice is sufficient time to see what have been the most enduring ideas that underpin David Morley Architects' portfolio, but this is not a retrospective book. By focussing on five themes, rather than a chronological sequence of projects, the ambition of this book is to establish a platform from which to build for the next 25 years.

The first theme explores the two ways in which new ideas can be developed, either through evolution or revolution. Are they mutually exclusive or is there a form of architecture which wholeheartedly embraces both? This leads on to a chapter about the importance of designing in accordance with nature and reflects on the consequences of that, not just in terms of the necessity to take care of the environment but also in generating designs which people feel comfortable with. Everything we do, ultimately, becomes enshrined in a geometric form and we have developed ideas for working in more than the traditional two and three dimensions. This culminates in thinking about a fifth dimension of geometry and considering the underlying geometric patterns which invoke an emotional response. The fourth theme is about process and how, through the act of tuning in, design can be targeted very specifically at a product that is focussed on the future needs of society. The final chapter discusses the principle of integration, seeking one idea to solve several different problems.

It emerges that all of the chapters are closely interrelated—although the book illustrates 25 projects, organised into five themes, in reality, any of the projects could have been illustrated in any of the chapters. We are very fortunate to be able to publish personal introductions to each of the five chapters from an august selection of architects, engineers, clients and critics.

The book title comes from the terminology from voice communications protocols, where the signal quality is reported on two scales: the first for signal strength, the second for signal clarity. These scales range from one to five, where one is the worst and five is the best. The listening station reports these numbers separated with the word "by". "Five by 5" therefore means a signal that has excellent strength and perfect clarity—the most understandable signal possible. We believe that is a good target for many aspects of architecture. Readers will be familiar with the five bar scale on their cell phones and scientists with the concept of the five-sigma level of certainty. "Five by 5" expresses the importance given to dialogue and communication in David Morley Architects' design approach. So the designs and ideas that are illustrated here are the product of teamwork, from a cherished pool of in-house designers, managed by my business partner Andy Mytom, through to a broad range of consultants and contractors who we enjoy working with. However at the head of the team are the people that enable us to do our best work—our much valued clients.

DAVID MORLEY

OPPOSITE
Solar shades at Plymouth University's Rolle Building.

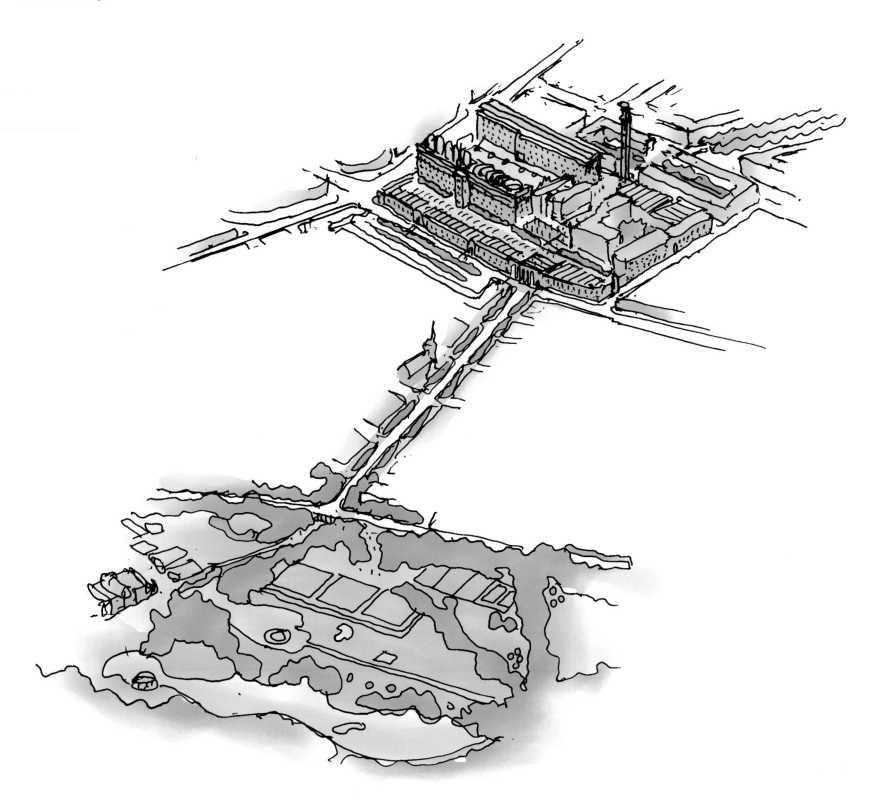

For a long time I have been a great believer in metamorphosis—and in every field we do not inhabit anything that was left as God left it. So what was a progressive or 'blue sky thinking' element last year becomes part of the vernacular by next year. Even if you went into traditional architecture it would be difficult to say what is good honest traditional technique. My own use of the word "vernacular" sometimes upsets those people who use vernacular as a sort of protective thing—"It ought to be designed in the vernacular" meaning an agreed upon revivalist aesthetic, but I interpret vernacular meaning that it becomes part of the way that you do something.

Taking buildings of the late nineteenth and early twentieth century and then adding the potential of new techniques and technologies, may look surprising because their mannerisms are mixed, in the same way that the first people that wore plastic rain coats looked odd and shiny and strange, but in fact as raincoats they did a slightly better job for the purpose than something woven out of cloth. I think the same thing happens with David Morley Architects' buildings. I look at the Lister Mills scheme and then the building that the new part sits upon which is four square with the odd turret to decorate it. The new objects look upon first sight as if they have landed from outer space, but actually on second sight they have not but are in fact pods or cabins using current technology. You could elaborate the argument and say that they in themselves are in the tradition of the mansard roof, (which itself was an invention for tax purposes to make possible the addition to a four square building). So evolution and revolution can often run in strange circular patterns.

I wrote in *Spirit and Invention*, that David's work, while having the clarity of approach and professionalism that one would expect, given his academic and working background, at the same time showed a level of wit (quietly stated) and inventiveness that inevitably took one by surprise.[1] So, for example, the atrium slot inserted into Velvet Mill becomes almost like delicate surgery. This is interesting because there are many parallels—if you send a car into the garage and it has a new engine put in it, where is the spirit of the car? Is it in the engine because it's the most important part? Or is it in the shell? There need be only one fundamental addition or insertion and the whole way you think about a building changes. Sometimes there is a turnover point—although there may be an underlying DNA, yet suddenly there is a very different proposition.

Another issue is the enjoyment of technology. There are some people under the erroneous view that they are either technical types or art types and, although David and I are of slightly different generations, we both subscribe to the fact that it is technology that has enabled art to revivify the world of architecture. When Colin Fournier and I made our building in Graz that has pixelations of light, the fact that this was achieved with ordinary fittings and therefore it was economic became a double delight. Appropriation and then the delight in the appropriation. The Austrians in general have a natural and long craft tradition. There is still this enjoyment of things and bits, a certain perverseness that somebody like Hoffmann, (who David refers to later), indulged, but the point is that he and people like him knew when it was pointless to push the physiognomy of a functioning object. If the spoon will not go in the mouth, then it is not working as a spoon, and there are many spoons that you can go and buy in art gallery gift shops that just don't operate as a spoon.

PETER COOK

1. *Spirit and Invention*, London: Architectural Association, 1982.

PREVIOUS PAGES
David Morley Architects' proposals for Velvet Mill form the second phase of development of Lister Mills by Urban Splash.

OPPOSITE
The Lister Mills development is planned to be a catalyst for the regeneration of Manningham in Bradford.

Each of the 25 projects illustrated in this book has been designed to modify the environment in some way. Whether this happens by evolution, by revolution, or by both evolution and revolution is the subject of this chapter. The analogy of evolution in architecture compared to evolution in biology is explored in Philip Steadman's book *The Evolution of Designs*, where he distinguishes between Darwin's and Lavarack's theories of evolution, the former proposing evolution through natural selection and the second through organisms adapting to new environmental conditions. Here, evolution is taken as meaning gradual change based on precedent, as opposed to revolution which means sudden change without reference to the past.

Many design factors today are the same as they were in the past, for example: the trajectory of the sun across the sky, the general shape of the human body and the environmental conditions required to be fairly comfortable. There is therefore scope to consider how architecture in the past has responded to those consistent factors, almost as the 'DNA' from which a new architecture can evolve. Likewise, through a process of cross-fertilisation, there is the potential to bring existing ideas into a new context and thereby introduce fresh new thinking through an evolutionary process. On the other hand revolutionary change can occur through simple invention, having an original idea or by finding a completely new way of solving a problem. Alternatively, revolutionary change can happen by exploiting technological developments to create something which wasn't previously possible. A common driver for change, whether it be evolutionary or revolutionary is the need to respond to the changing needs of society and solve new problems that didn't exist before. For example, the Velvet Mill project, featured later in this chapter, evolves from the existing fabric of the building to give it a completely new use responding to a social need for urban regeneration, bringing a revolutionary approach to the roofscape, exploiting a new building technology and giving expression to the future ambitions of the city.

This interplay between evolution and revolution is elegantly illustrated by the simple design of a spoon by the architect Josef Hoffmann (1870–1956) in 1904. The evolutionary aspect of contemporary design is to recognise the value of solutions that have developed over time and are as relevant today as they were when they were first developed. Thus the mouth piece of the spoon is very traditional in shape. However, a freshness of approach can be achieved by exploring appropriate new technologies or solving new problems that didn't exist before. In this example it was the new process of hot forging stainless steel that enabled Hoffman to give the spoon an extremely slender stem which is then counterbalanced by a graceful circular droplet.

During that period, around the turn of the twentieth century, the rapid technological and social change generated a branching out of approaches to architecture which remains apparent today. The one thing in common was an appetite for a new approach evident in similar descriptions for distinctly different approaches, such as Art Nouveau and Esprit Nouveau—the former promoting a more evolutionary approach to design and the latter a more revolutionary approach. Somewhere in between is the work of the Ecole de Nancy. Just three years before Hoffmann's spoon design, the architect George Biet (1869–1955) designed an exquisite cafe known as *La Cure d'Air Trianon* in Nancy. The building has sadly fallen into disrepair but still demonstrates how something startlingly original can come from exploring new technologies, in this case the use of iron in domestic architecture. In the 1976 retrospective exhibition Nancy 1900, F Charpentier notes that "Individualism—a characteristic of the nineteenth century—actualised a common yearning after differences", this seems as relevant today as it was then and indeed, since then, a tradition of innovative design can be seen in Nancy through the work of Victor Prouvé and his son Jean Prouvé. Because their work was strongly derived from the craft of making things, yet also pioneered the use of emerging new technologies, it has illustrated a harmonious combination of both evolution and revolution.

OPPOSITE
View of Velvet Mill from Manningham, Bradford.

ABOVE
Spoon design by Josef Hoffmann.

LEFT
View of the bar at the Lord's Indoor School.

RIGHT
A notable detail at the *La Cure d'Air Trianon*
is the way the terracotta block floors make
use of the two natural colours of clay and are
simply expressed giving a decorative effect
which inspired the soffit treatment at the
Lord's Indoor School.

OPPOSITE LEFT
Entrance Canopy at the Hospital of St John
and St Elizabeth.

OPPOSITE RIGHT
West elevation of the Hospital of St John
and St Elizabeth.

David Morley Architects' first built project, completed in 1989, illustrates
how evolutionary and revolutionary developments were integrated in the
design. The Hospital of St John and St Elizabeth is an acute hospital in
the St John's Wood conservation area of London, set amongst Georgian
stucco villas in mature gardens. Morley's project was to replace an existing
Victorian villa with a building which would provide a new hospital entrance
and reception, out-patients and in-patients facilities and an imaging
department. The first point of difference is the window design. All of the
contemporary precedents for this building type had, at that time, been
designed with horizontal bands of ribbon windows. The ribbon window
offers some benefits in terms of flexibility to locate partition walls, but
its initial popularity stemmed from a fashionable architectural style. The
modern movement rejected tall vertical windows because they were seen
as synonymous with an out of date load bearing form of construction. The

horizontal ribbon window was seen by architects as an honest expression
of the potential of the structural frame. Notably the "*fenetre en longeur*"
was one of Le Corbusier's "*Cinq points d'une architecture nouvelle*".[1] Although
the Hospital of St John and St Elizabeth is a concrete frame building,
horizontal windows were not used. Instead, very tall vertical windows were
proposed because they provide the most efficient means of maximising
light penetration to the perimeter bedrooms. They also give a patient in
bed a view of the ground and the sky with excellent opportunities for low
level and high level openings, allowing all perimeter spaces to be naturally
ventilated. Like the mouth piece of Hoffman's spoon, the traditional shape
of the window is a natural evolution of a traditional model exemplified
by Georgian style houses and the added bonus of this approach was to
establish proportional relationships with the adjacent Georgian villas. This
relationship was reinforced by making the exterior cladding a precise colour

match to the neighbouring properties. The approach here was not to be revolutionary for the sake of it, but to evolve traditional models where they are useful and appropriate. However, the concept for the cladding itself was revolutionary because, for the first time ever in England, it used an external insulated render system to provide a highly insulated jacket around the high thermal mass concrete and block structure, reducing thermal swing and consequent energy loads.

The entrance canopy has been used as a visual device for making the hospital's purpose legible as well as providing shelter for visitors arriving. This is discussed later in this book in "Tuning In". The canopy design here is evolutionary since it was inspired by Jean Prouvé's *Maison du Peuple* in Clichy, 1939, and was developed as a means of transferring a cantilever into a concrete frame with two simple point loads.

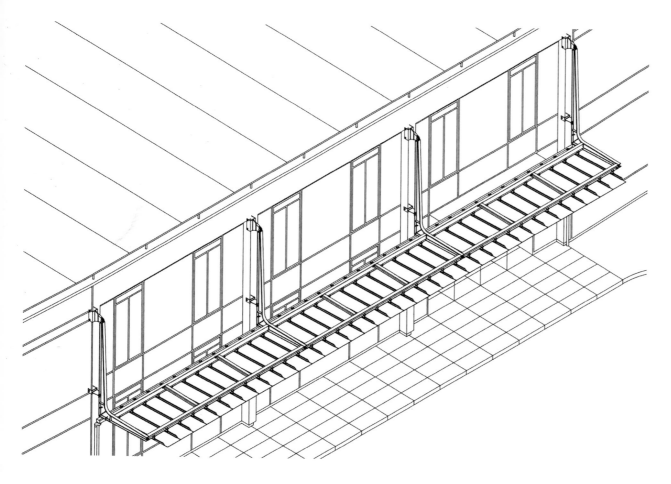

LEFT
Structural diagram for the entrance canopy.

RIGHT
Maison du Peuple, Jean Prouve, 1939.

In acute healthcare facilities the technical equipment can be a disproportionately significant investment yet also subject to more rapid technological development and change. So the versatility of the structure to accommodate new layouts derived from new ways of treating patients is paramount. At the **Hospital of St John and St Elizabeth** this is facilitated by a simple plan comprising three by five structural bays with a race track of services around the central three bays which has given ample flexibility for future layout changes and has also allowed perimeter spaces to be either naturally or mechanically ventilated. The structure was also designed to allow expansion upwards. In this sense a healthcare building needs to accommodate both evolution and revolution in response to an evolving programme of use during the design life and also revolutions in the way patients can be treated.

One of the revolutions in the United Kingdom's National Health Service (NHS) has been the concept of bringing healthcare to the high street with facilities where patients can drop-in without an appointment. In response to this trend, a concept for a Walk-In Centre was pioneered with a building which David Morley Architects converted in Luton in 2004.

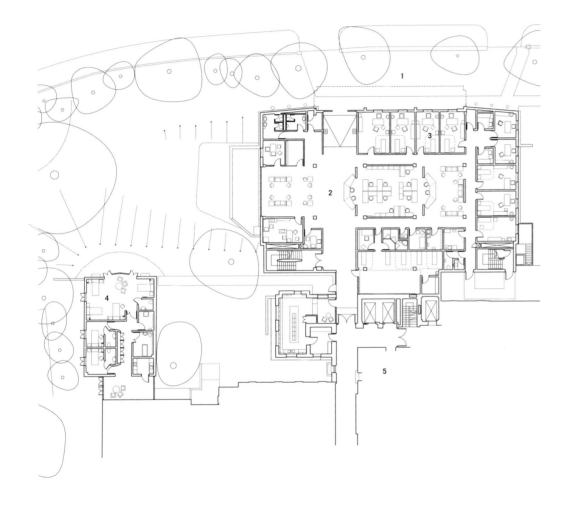

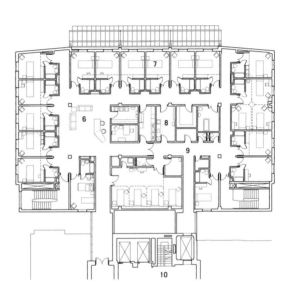

LEFT
Ground floor plan.
1 Drop-off
2 Reception
3 Consulting rooms
4 Hospice
5 Existing hospital

RIGHT
First floor plan.
6 Nurse base
7 Bedrooms
8 Utility areas
9 Service and Circulation 'race track'
10 Existing hospital

LEFT
Existing building before.

RIGHT
Double-height entrance area.

OPPOSITE LEFT
Detail of the facade.

OPPOSITE RIGHT
Street frontage of Luton Walk-In Centre.

Luton Primary Care Trust wanted a building that would be entirely accessible to the local population: inviting without being exposed, clean and modern but not 'clinical', and compact, as it was to occupy an existing building in a tight high street location. After an extensive search the chosen building was in an ideal location, but required extensive refurbishment to become the facility that was needed. To gain internal space the envelope was extended to the boundaries of the site. At the front, a glass facade was added bringing public areas to the pavement edge in a light, unimposing way, and giving full visibility to the waiting areas on ground and first floors. An outer 'layer' to the facade comprising a canopy, vertical supports and grillage to the upper windows—all constructed in galvanised steel, provides shade to the south-facing elevation and gives a fresh new image to a previously tired and ungainly building. Inside, materials and colours were selected to give the **Luton Walk-In Centre** vibrant highlights within

a generally calming atmosphere. They are also robust and easy to clean. The reception desk is strategically located for good visibility without being confrontational, and affording some privacy to visitors.

Since opening, the Centre has been extremely busy. Visitors are able to walk in off the street, they don't have to be registered with the NHS, and the Centre is open until ten o'clock in the evening every day. All of these features enhance its appeal. Luton has pockets of severe deprivation, and access to public healthcare is not always easy. The new Centre takes pressure off the other facilities and attracts patients that have traditionally felt alienated from the system—for example, Asian women, local sex workers, and refugees.

So on some occasions the brief for a project demands a new prototype to be developed. On other occasions new prototypes can emerge simply

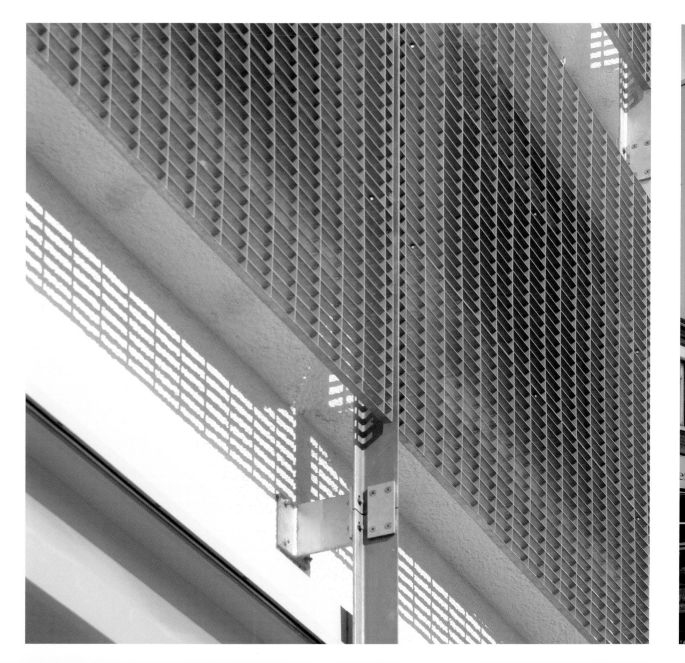

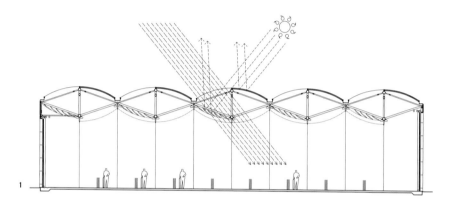

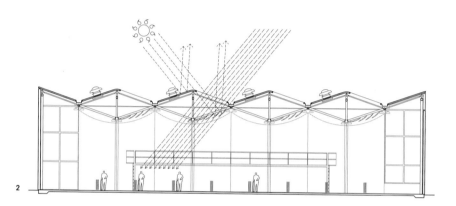

by discovering a better way to accommodate a client's needs than had ever previously been imagined. Later in this book, in "Natural Consequences", the way buildings adapt to the natural elements is discussed. Whilst one would expect this to be an evolutionary process, because natural forces change only gradually, there is potential for revolution to occur through new ways of thinking to generate originality, even if the nature of the problem being tackled and the technologies applied already exist. By way of example, the succession of indoor cricket schools designed by David Morley Architects began with a simple idea, which was revolutionary at the time, to find a way of reconciling abundant daylight in a building whilst avoiding any problems of sudden variations in light levels or of overheating through solar gain.

This began with the competition winning scheme for the Marylebone Cricket Club's new **Lord's Indoor Cricket School** at Lord's Ground in London, completed in 1994. Having invented a successful revolutionary prototype, for such a prestigious client, it was found that other cricket clubs wanted a simple copy. So Charpentier's observation about a "common yearning after differences" ceases to apply when something new and desirable has just been invented. The second example was built

for **Warwickshire County Cricket Club** at Edgbaston and was completed in 2000.[2] This lottery funded scheme had an even more demanding budget and some evolution was required to explore how the daylight solution at Lord's could be delivered in a more economic form. The structural grid was refined thereby reducing the steel weight from 60kg / m^2 to 56kg / m^2. The curved barrel vaults were replaced with a flat panel system that produced some significant savings and echoed the more industrial heritage of the region. The palette of materials was extended using etched terracotta panels on the street facade resulting from collaboration with the adjacent Midland Arts Centre, to make this the first contemporary building on Birmingham's Terracotta Trail. Three further cricket centres followed, each one of which has evolved the principles established at the Lord's Indoor School in response to a slightly different context. At Chester-le-Street and South Northumberland a smaller building was required which needed to be linked to the existing adjacent pavilions and at the National Cricket Academy at Loughborough, a longer building was proposed, to allow for wicket keepers to stand back behind the batsmen, but in each evolution, gradual improvements were made to environmental control and economy. The steel weight was eventually reduced to just 45kg / m^2.

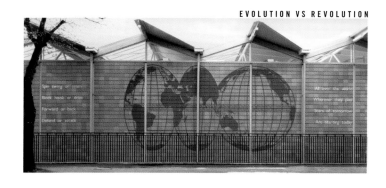

LEFT
View of the indoor nets at Edgbaston.

TOP RIGHT
Detail of the integrated art on the terracotta facade.

BOTTOM RIGHT
At the Edgbaston Indoor Cricket School, the side panels of the facade can be retracted to provide summer time ventilation and access for setting up major events.

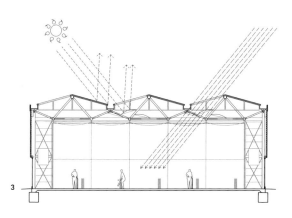

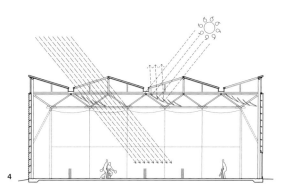

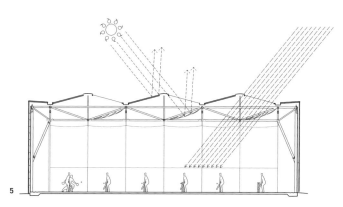

3

4

5

LEFT
The elevation facing the main cricket ground is clad in green oak to resist cricket ball impact—this facade faces northeast and so can include glazing in the form of patio doors at the base to provide a visual link but is also part of a ventilation strategy connected with automatically opening rooflights.

OPPOSITE
At the National Cricket Academy the site levels are exploited to enter the pavilion at mid-level where there is a reception and teaching spaces. Changing is below and viewing terraces are above.

RIGHT
The artificial light is brought on automatically using digital ballasts as daylight fades—a technology that was not available when the first generation cricket school at Lord's was constructed.

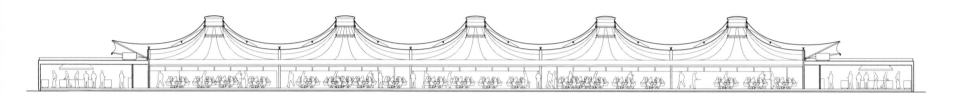

ABOVE
Section through the Nursery Pavilion.

OPPOSITE
View of the Nursery Pavilion from the Indoor
Cricket School.

Cricket grounds have historically been busy places in the summer months and quieter in the winter and thus, at Lord's Ground, an extensive array of temporary structures were brought in for just six months of the year and then taken away. However, the financial pressure on sports grounds is now such that an all year round use needs to be considered. The **Nursery Pavilion** at Lord's, completed in 1999, replaces the need for the flappy marquees that were erected and dismantled every cricket season to provide facilities for hospitality. It also creates a structure which can be used throughout the year for other purposes such as training, banqueting and exhibitions. The accommodation provides space for 1,000 covers in a restaurant configuration, and can be converted to a theatre-style layout for 400 with separate seated banqueting or can be sub-divided into hospitality boxes. The site comprised an existing tarmac car park adjacent to the Nursery Ground above an underground railway which determined a maximum zone of 450 millimetres deep for all foundations and drainage. The ground slopes evenly along its length, with an overall change in level of 1.5 metres.

To take advantage of the good views, the building stretches along the full length of the Nursery Ground. There are three key elements, a main hall and two service modules providing space for the kitchens, WCs and plant. The whole is covered with a white fabric roof which reinforces the 'village green' character at Lord's, cross-referencing the tented roof of Michael Hopkins' Mound Stand. But here, for all year round environmental control, there is a double-skin fabric membrane and the supporting structure for the roof is integrated within it, giving an overall appearance of the building being low-key in relation to the principal match ground buildings. In order to avoid extensive flights of steps the entire building is set at a 1:65 gradient, a quietly revolutionary idea, since nobody, other than the architects ever notices it. To eliminate foundations to the central area, the floor is made from a simple office raised floor system, propped off the existing tarmac car park, easily re-locatable and easy to adjust if there is any ground settlement in the future.

In each bay, a cranked pyramid of steelwork provides a push-up support for each of the computer generated PVC membrane flourotops, making this a contemporary tent shape that could not have been conceived without that technology. A two and a half metre wide canopy provides shelter and shade to the west elevation. The fabric structure is pulled down adjacent to the columns to provide drainage points to prevent overflow of water onto the Nursery Ground adapting a revolutionary siphonic rainwater system first developed in Sweden which allows larger quantities of water to discharge through smaller bore pipes without the need for any drainage falls.

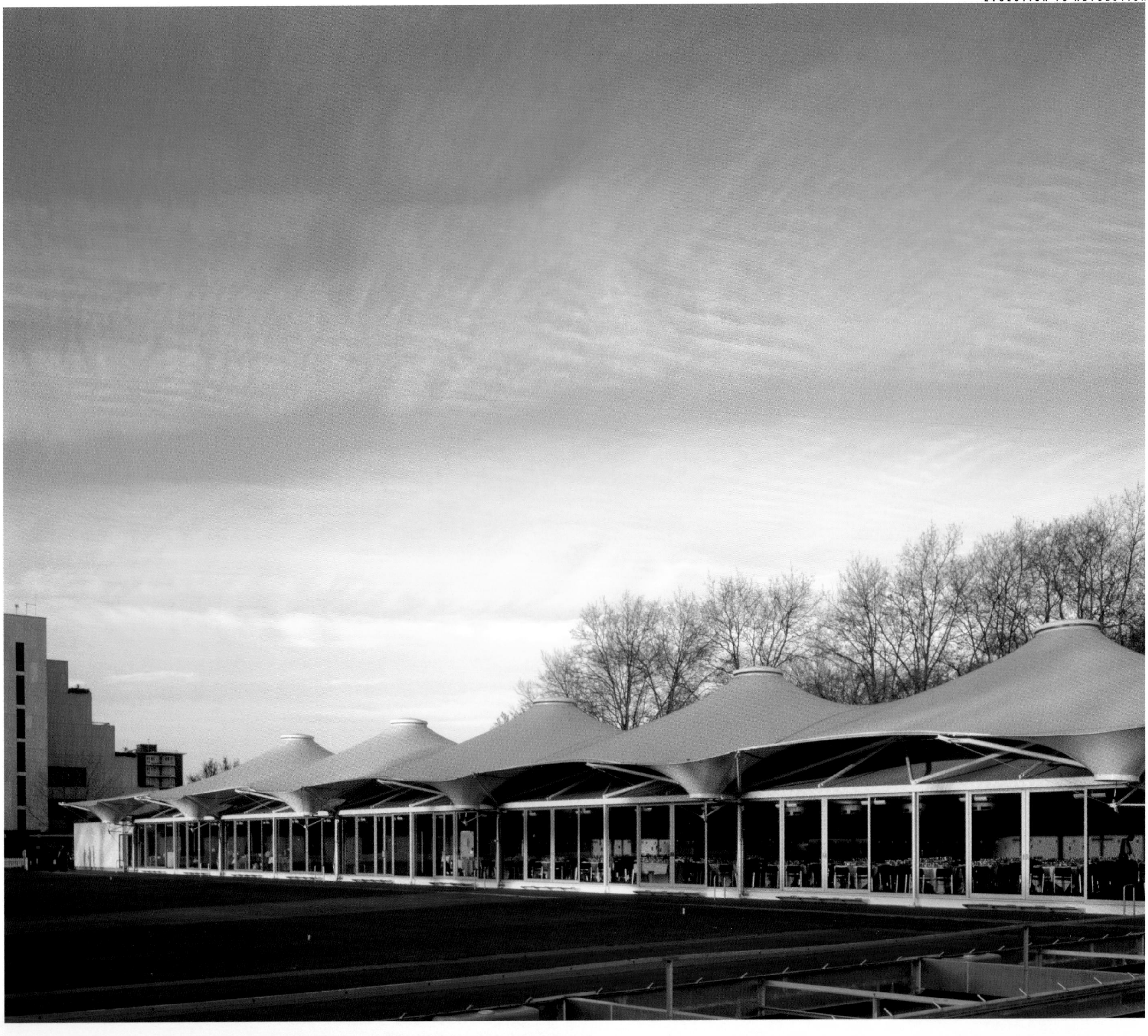

LEFT
View of the Nursery End at Lord's Ground showing the Nursery Pavilion on the left, adjacent to the Indoor Cricket School, the England and Wales Cricket Board Headquarters and the Lord's Shop (featured in the "Natural Consequences" and "Tuning In" chapters).

RIGHT
Interior view showing the Nursery Pavilion laid out for a banquet.

The Nursery Pavilion is an evolution of a marquee. It can survive the winter weather because the fabric uses high performance insulating materials and the double curvature of the computer generated form prevents it from flapping in high winds. So it is revolutionary as well, deploying new technologies and responding to the societal need for sports grounds to have a more sustainable use. This combination of evolution and revolution allows a new building to be anchored into a traditional context. For example, in nearby Regent's Park, the 'Hub' featured in the next chapter, is a contemporary version of John

Nash's concept for buildings to be ornaments in the park. In London's Hyde Park, Morley's yet to be realised proposals for Marlborough Gate will create a contemporary alcove adjacent to Christopher Wren's Queen Anne Alcove to form a new cafe, park entrance and backdrop to the heritage Italian Gardens. In the same way as it has worked in parks, this combination of both evolution and revolution seems to be fruitful for regenerating cities—by evolution, engaging with the existing fabric and through revolution, promoting new optimistic opportunities for living.

LEFT
Detail of the canopy and siphonic drainage.

TOP RIGHT
Model of proposals to remodel Marlborough
Gate in Hyde Park.

BOTTOM RIGHT
The Hub in Regent's Park.

Velvet Mill was part of a fantastically robust complex of derelict weaving mills in a formerly deprived area of Bradford in the north of England but now a major focus of regeneration being led by developers Urban Splash in conjunction with Bradford City Council and Yorkshire Forward. Although built for an industrial use, the setting is really quite palatial. Everything is generous—the Mill Buildings are as long and tall as Buckingham Palace in London and the boiler house chimney is like an Italian campanile though much higher at 76 metres tall. Velvet Mill is the grandest of the Mills with 4.3 metre floor to floor heights, it is 108 metres long and has a massive overhanging stone dentil breaking cornice and a boldly projecting French pavilion slate roof on top of the central tower. The buildings were commissioned by Samuel Lister in 1873 who was a great innovator, securing more United Kingdom patents than any of his contemporaries, and there was an opportunity to extend that tradition of innovation into the refurbishment and extension of Velvet Mill.

The most dramatic change was to give a new life to a building that had been neglected and unloved for almost 40 years. The handsome stonework was cleaned up and repaired and the window openings were retained but with new windows that respected the original design philosophy by minimising the intrusion of metal frames and maximising the penetration of daylight using the high floor to ceiling heights.

The fifth floor posed some problems for the refurbishment because it was originally toplit and had no windows. However, it became possible to discreetly create new window openings in between the massive stone dentils that ran right through the full thickness of the wall with a ready-made stone lining. Overall there are 190 apartments, with community and commercial space at ground floor level. The central grand staircase was restored to become the main circulation core and a new full-height atrium was created to bring lots of light through from the roof and link the entrance to a suite of new penthouses that have been created on the roof. The roof of Velvet Mill is a special place. From it, one can see for miles around, there are great diagonal views to the Yorkshire Moors to the northeast and to the northwest, back to Bradford Centre. Of course, that also means that you get views of the roof from some distant viewpoints so there was an opportunity for the roofscape to become a beacon signalling the regeneration of this quarter of Bradford.

The roof structure is like a curvilinear metal fabric wrapped into a plait. At the fold lines the fabric is cut away to create windows and balconies with glass slots for the staircases. This generates a rigorous geometry which harmonises with the structure below and creates space for some generous two-storey apartments that face out diagonally towards the long views. Because the Mill is such a robust massive building the roof structure was made to be light and delicate and of sufficient scale not to become confused with the heavily articulated profile of the stone parapet. From close to, because it is set back behind the parapet it is quite unobtrusive but from a distance the plait-like appearance of the roof is more legible evoking imagery of both the tradition of weaving and the process of regeneration.

The roof has been sculpted using revolutionary 3-D computer software that didn't exist before the twenty-first century and so it is a truly contemporary design; the materials used reflect this—natural zinc metal finish for the roof, facetted glazing for the stair slots, generous glass doors leading to timber decked balconies and terraces—these are all very light and delicate to complement the massive stone structure below.

All these projects have an evolutionary element, through a development of the existing building fabric or cross-fertilisation of existing precedents and ideas, and they all have a revolutionary element through finding a new way of solving a problem or deploying a recently emerging technology.

OPPOSITE LEFT
Main entrance at Velvet Mill.

OPPOSITE RIGHT
Aerial view of Velvet Mill.

TOP
Model showing concept for the penthouses.

BOTTOM
View of typical apartment.

RIGHT
View of the proposed penthouse. The scheme for Velvet Mill has a sort of inevitability about it, it is finely tuned and is a logical extension of what is currently there, working with the grain in a way that perhaps Samuel Lister, if he had been here today, would have wholeheartedly supported.

OPPOSITE LEFT
The structure of the penthouses is made from double-curved timber cassettes made from a framework of curved Oriented Strand Board (OSB) and plywood ribs with OSB outer lining panels, forming a shell that spans between two steel hoops. The 300 millimetre deep space between the ribs is packed with insulation and the faceted outer panel surface is sheathed with a breather membrane and then cross-lined diagonally with timber boarding on battens. This evens out the facets and forms the double-curved surface to take the zinc pre-patinated roof covering and also creates a ventilated zone underneath.

OPPOSITE RIGHT
Integrating Evolution and Revolution.

'MAKING A DIFFERENCE'

EVOLUTION

REVOLUTION

DNA

CROSS - FERTILISATION

TECHNOLOGICAL CHANGE

INVENTION

They are also all projects that are directed towards a purpose relating to the evolving needs of society, whether it is in delivering better healthcare, more sustainable buildings or helping a process of urban regeneration.

In each case, the evolutionary aspect has been to recognise that there are existing solutions that are as relevant today as they were in the past and that by freely learning from that, new buildings become naturally rooted in their physical and historical context. However, evolution can go hand in hand with revolution. Whereas in the twentieth century, when revolutionary ideas served to

disconnect architecture from its context, causing old ideas to be ignored simply because they were not new, in the twenty-first century there is an opportunity to integrate revolution with evolution, building on tradition in a contemporary way, to make a difference, not just for the sake of making a difference.

1. Le Corbusier and Jeanneret, P, "*Cinq points d'une architecture nouvelle*", *Die Form*, vol 2, 1972.

2. Edgbaston Cricket School was in association with BPN Architects.

Natural. It is a word with many connotations. We see it used in the promotion of food, holidays, clothing, medicine and more. It represents simplicity and the elemental. We associate it with performers, sportspeople and speakers; those that have an easy way with skills that many of us find to be fraught, even frightening. In whatever way we use the word, we almost always do a disservice to the process, the thought, the creativity, the imagination and the hours of diligent hard work required to deliver what appears 'natural'.

This chapter embraces the notion as concentrating natural forces in a relaxed fashion.

It is a view of design that I share; one that starts with the entire universe of possibility and quickly narrows to the challenge at hand. We can start with everything imaginable and available, and strip it back to the solar system, that which circles the sun. Further reduction restricts our considerations to the earth, at the top of our atmosphere. This restriction of the boundary leaves us solar radiation as energy and rejects the same quantity of energy from other radiation outwards to the universe. This last part of the process is essential to the understanding of global warming but is not essential for the day-to-day design of buildings.

The essences of building design are related to the subjective perceptions of people and the physical realities of the building in its surrounds. Extremely sensational or whimsical values are not given a heavy weight in the buildings chosen for study in this chapter. The physical relationships of the building to its environment are taken more seriously, leading to an emphasis on environmental and social sustainability.

The Indoor Cricket School at Lord's was a project secured by way of design competition, and is illustrative of David Morley's approach. He invited structural and environmental engineers to join the design process at the very beginning. Competitions are usually carried out very quickly, and the concentration of thought and investigation is sharpened as a result. The team met on the first morning and agreed that natural lighting in the cricket centre should be adequate for play on a cloudy day. We considered a saw-tooth north-light roof but the geometry did not capture sufficient daylight. The meeting broke up on Saturday morning and by mid-morning Sunday, David had devised a synthesis that solved the problem. He put it to me and I agreed it was likely to work. I hope he remembers that I congratulated him for creating this solution! You'll read about what David created and how it works in this chapter, but I want to highlight how nature informs the design process. The building develops as a natural consequence of natural forces. In this way, buildings can be outstandingly sustainable without making a display of quirky 'sustainable' features.

MAX FORDHAM

PREVIOUS PAGES
The Hub forms part of a master plan that has restored the balance between sport and nature in Regent's Park, London.

OPPOSITE
The analogy with trees and plants has closely informed some of the practice's designs, such as this detail of the Isis Education Centre in Hyde Park, London.

The Oxford English Dictionary defines the word natural in two ways. First as "in accordance with nature" and second as "relaxed and unaffected". These definitions encapsulate two distinctly different but closely interrelated aspects of David Morley Architects' design approach. "In accordance with nature" has been taken to mean how the elements of nature inform design (for example sunlight, daylight, fresh air) and "relaxed and unaffected" has been taken to mean designs that are not wilful, that are aimed to be the inevitable consequence of the needs of the client, the users, society generally and the environmental conditions.

There is much to learn from nature about what makes good design. Take trees for example. They are rooted elegantly in the earth, they have economic structures, they help purify the air, they gather energy from the sun, create shade and shelter, respond to orientation and are instrumental in combatting climate change. All of the natural elements are important for us: earth, air and sky, plants and water. This chapter explores how an architecture that responds to these natural elements for the benefit of society is also an architecture that is relaxed and unaffected.

The earth is a good place to start from since that is where the construction process begins. The potential of building with earth was explored at the **Regent's Park Hub**, completed in 2005. After the Second World War, Regent's Park became a depository for much of London's bomb rubble. This was used to flatten out the once undulating landscape of the Northern Parklands that John Nash (1752–1835) had designed and create in its

place an extensive area of sports pitches. Unfortunately the clay capping that was used led to some major drainage problems and the pitches could therefore not be used intensively. The northern parklands had also become criss-crossed by open pathways forcing an inefficient layout of pitches, many with incorrect orientation to the sun. The layout of pitches right across the park also detracted from the other aspects the park needed to deliver in terms of ecology and non-sport recreation. The Regent's Park project began as an exercise in renovating the vast expanse of earth which makes up the northern parkland, re-planning the paths, reconfiguring the pitches and installing new drainage and irrigation. This allowed a more compact arrangement for formal sport, whilst still achieving increased use, freeing up substantial new areas to give a more ecologically rich landscape for the enjoyment of non-sports users and creating new wild-life habitats. The sports pitches were previously served by a pavilion, built in the 1960s and hidden in the trees, which was suffering structural defects and wasn't compatible with the Royal Parks' objectives to increase accessibility to the several areas of deprived communities located nearby. Rather than rebuild the pavilion on the existing site a new location was proposed which would be more accessible and closer to the centre of gravity of sports activity. The site was carefully chosen to maximise the Hub's visibility as a point of orientation and the sensitivity of the setting in the heritage landscape was tested with full-scale mock-ups of the proposed building outline. The access path was benched into the ground so that from afar the Hub appears to be floating in a sea of grass with a backdrop of trees which helps to anchor it in the landscape.

OPPOSITE
Regent's Park, London.

LEFT
Sketch prepared for the competitive interview showing the idea of a pavilion that would appear to have the scale of a bandstand and build on John Nash's concept that the buildings in Regent's Park should appear as ornaments in the park.

RIGHT
Bomb rubble being extracted from the site of the Regent's Park Hub.

TOP LEFT
A four metre diameter rooflight is formed
from an ETFE cushion combining good
daylight penetration and insulation.

BOTTOM LEFT
A rooflight above the stair allows light to
flood to the lower level.

RIGHT
1   Entrance
2   Changing rooms
3   Cafe
4   Terrace
5   Rotunda

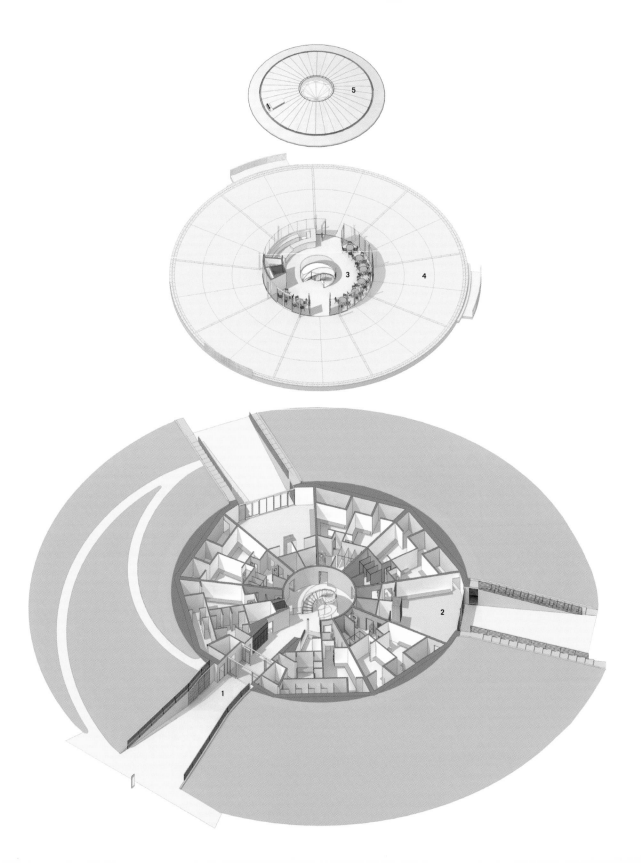

The building itself is quite large, providing changing space for 300 people, but the scale is concealed within an earth mound. The entrance is through a slice in the mound and the changing rooms are organised around a central rotunda so there are no corridors and it is easy to supervise. The rooms are planned to be flexible so they can be opened up in summer when there is lower demand and used as cricket pavilions or educational spaces. A stair spirals up through the central rotunda to the terrace above where there is a small cafe opening up onto a roof terrace, creating a 360 degree pavilion. The roof of the cafe is designed like a giant bicycle wheel, a very efficient form of structure where all the spokes of the wheel are in tension, supporting a central hub. Here the hub physically supports a central rooflight but also symbolises the purpose of the building as a focal point. This design led to the naming of the building as the Hub. Since then the word Hub has become extensively used throughout the country to describe buildings which provide a focus for the community.

The bicycle wheel roof structure is exposed in the cafe.

The beauty of surrounding the building with earth is that not only does it create viewing terraces and a place to sit and look out to the surrounding sports, but it also has some considerable environmental benefits.

There is a large difference in temperature above ground and below ground. Above ground it is in the range of zero to ten degrees centigrade in winter and ten to 20 degrees centigrade in the summer whereas below ground it is a stable ten degrees centigrade. So by surrounding the Hub with this thermal mass of earth, the building is kept warm in winter and cool in summer, which is a very simple way of reducing the energy costs and carbon dioxide emissions. Part of the "Natural Consequence" of the Hub is that the idea of the mound works in many different ways: it gives a recreational aspect, it reduces the visual bulk of the building and the way it sits in the landscape, and also offers a significant environmental benefit. There is massive potential to use the temperature differentials above and below ground to reduce society's reliance on fossil fuels.

OPPOSITE
The earth mound is constructed re-using bomb rubble and topsoil from excavation, the pitch improvement works, and the previously demolished pavilion—it reduces the visual bulk of what is quite a large building exposed in a heritage landscape.

ABOVE
Using the thermal mass of earth is a simple way of keeping buildings warm in winter and cool in summer.

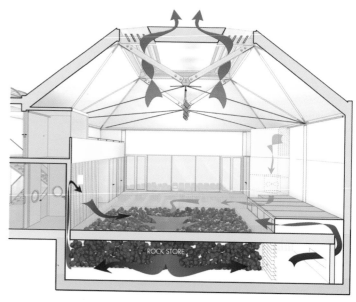

LEFT
The Centre for Two St James—the natural air vents are at high level on the left hand side.

RIGHT
Warm air from outside is drawn through the rock store at the Centre for Two St James, from natural buoyancy through acoustically attenuated extraction in the roof.

OPPOSITE
The hall in the Centre for Two St James showing the air vents by the stage and natural air extraction and natural light from above.

At the **Centre for Two St James** in Gerrard's Cross, completed in 2005, the space below the building was used to create a natural form of comfort cooling in summer and pre-heated air in winter. The 400 person hall would get very hot in summer if there was no cooling. The client was very interested in the idea of achieving cooling naturally. The proposed solution was to modify the air temperatures by using an underground rock store. Cool air is drawn through the rock store at night and during the day hall ventilation can draw on controlled parts of the rock store to deliver air at the required temperature. In its first very hot summer of opening a reduction of six degrees centigrade was achieved from outside air temperature to internal. The initial cost of the installation was similar to air-conditioning but the running costs and carbon dioxide emissions have been considerably reduced. Energy consumption is further reduced by ensuring that as far as possible the key spaces are naturally lit through windows or sky lights. This, as with many other David Morley Architects projects, is a building designed to optimise its connections with the earth and the sky.

OPPOSITE TOP
North-facing rooflights and glazing.

OPPOSITE BOTTOM
The Lee Valley Athletics Centre is strongly connected to the ground and the sky.

BELOW
Cross-section through the Lee Valley Athletics Centre—thermal mass is provided by the ground, seating tiers, side walls and sprint track roof.

1 200 metre indoor track
2 Pole vault area
3 Sprint track
4 Ancillary accommodation
5 Natural ventilation extract and platform for solar collectors

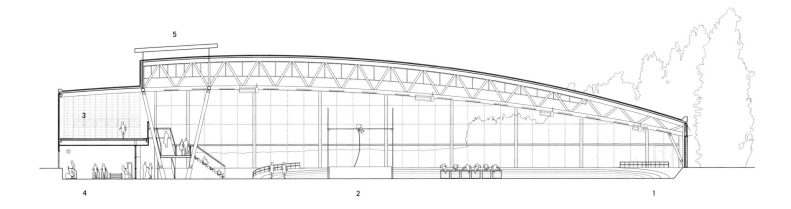

At the **Lee Valley Athletics Centre**, completed in 2007, the indoor track is partially dug into the earth. The usual way of constructing the banked corners needed for a 200 metre track is to raise them up above ground level, but this creates a visual obstruction in the floor plan. Here, the top of the banked corners are at ground level and the track is cut into the ground producing a bowl-like effect which is then exploited to create tiers of seating for spectators. The concrete seating steps and contact with the earth provides valuable thermal mass which helps prevent the building overheating in the summer. In the same way that contact with the earth helps moderate temperature and save energy, contact with the sky provides the means to bring in daylight, also saving energy and creating an uplifting environment. At Lee Valley, a single roof sweeps from a high point above the pole vault area to a low point determined by the requirements of running and hurdles. Orientation to the sun is very important and by planning the building on a north-south axis it became possible to prise open the roof to allow in daylight from the north but block out unwanted heat from solar radiation. The orientation also made it easy to fully glaze the end walls since it is easy to shade a south-facing facade and unnecessary to shade a north-facing facade. This allows the public to look in and creates a strong visual link between the inside and outside facilities. The columns rake out at an angle. This reduces the span of the roof and provides stability, eliminating the need for cross-bracing. The raking profile of the columns is like the arms of an athlete thrown up into the air as if in celebration.

This project illustrates design as a "Natural Consequence" in three ways. Firstly, the design is efficient and saves energy. Second, is that, although the procurement process was design and build and heavily cost driven, the project was not compromised because each of its parts are interdependent and fulfil a functional role such that they are already reduced to a minimum and cannot be value engineered. Third, is the positive feedback from athletes and visitors about the ambiance in the building. This was concisely expressed by the head of UK Athletics who said when he first came into the building that the atmosphere really made him want to get out there and run. What gives the building that character, the open plan feel, the bowl-like effect, the daylight and the structural form have all been derived from considerations of energy and efficiency. This is an example of how the character of a building can be natural and unaffected—a "Natural Consequence".

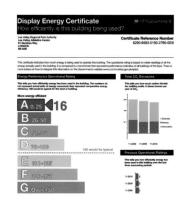

ABOVE
The overall effect of the energy saving is measured with a Display Energy Certificate score of A which is achieved only by the top one per cent of public buildings.

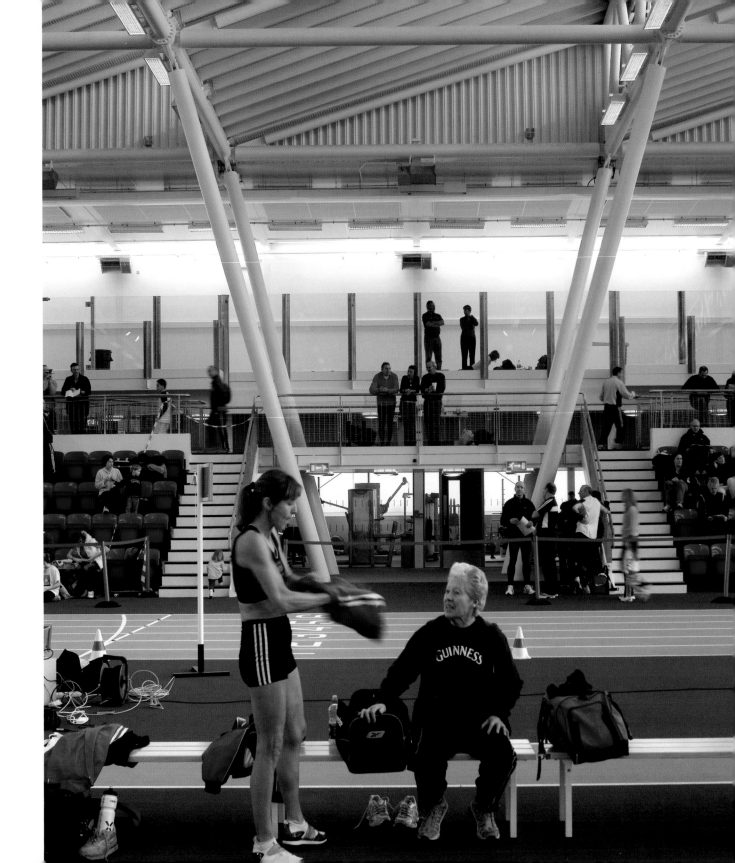

The upper level sprint track is accessed via scissor ramps with a half landing, framed by the splayed columns, providing a focal point on the centre line of the 200 metre track. The strength and conditioning suite is below the sprint track.

For many sports, and particularly for cricket, the quality of the playing surface, or earth, and the quality of light, or sky, are the two most important factors. Although the sky is highly predictable in terms of the sun location, weather conditions create significant variations in light levels which are difficult to predict. Such is the importance of the quality of light that all indoor cricket facilities used to be artificially lit in order to guarantee a completely uniform level of illumination. In 1993 the Marylebone Cricket Club (MCC) launched a competition for the new **Lord's Indoor Cricket School**. This gave Morley an opportunity to evolve from first principles a prototypical building which achieves uniform lighting using natural daylight. The competition-winning solution was so successful that it caused technical guidance notes to be re-written and was rolled out on many subsequent indoor cricket centres.

LEFT
The ancillary accommodation at the Lord's Indoor Cricket School forms a double-sided pavilion with views to both the indoor and outdoor cricket.

RIGHT
The sail cloth fabric louvres form miniature northlights that help scatter light up to the soffit to give a brightened appearance with no harsh contrasts.

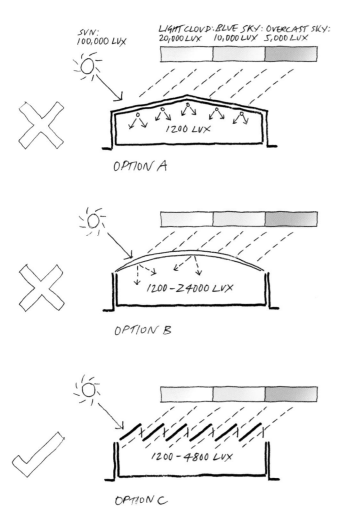

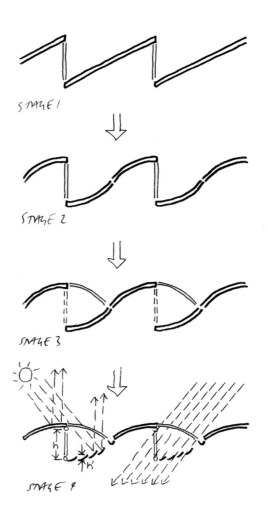

OPPOSITE
Between April and July the artificial lights are rarely used. In addition to the energy savings from lights, the annual close down for maintenance was extended from one to four years. The energy consumed has also been reduced by half, saving 351,650 kilowatt hours per year.

LEFT
Three options for lighting an indoor cricket centre:
Option A
- fluorescent light
- poor ambiance
- lighting consumes 250 kWh / m²
Option B
- fabric / translucent roof
- in bright sunlight 24,000 lux can quickly be reduced to 2,400 lux by a small cloud
Option C
- northlight roof
- only diffuse light admitted
- light level in excess of 1,200 lux except after sunset in winter
- no sudden variations in light level.

RIGHT
Development of the northlight concept to give better internal reflections, reducing glare, reduced external envelope and integration with the structure to support nets.
Stage 1: Traditional northlight roof
Stage 2: Softer form to give better internal reflections
Stage 3: Move glass line to reduce external envelope
Stage 4: Make inner layer from fabric louvres and increase the effective height of available northlight.

Indoor cricket requires a very high level of illumination, 2,000 lux, four times as much as most other sports. The traditional solution for artificially lit cricket centres was therefore very wasteful of energy since the light levels can vary from 5,000 lux for an overcast sky up to 100,000 lux in direct sunlight. However the solution was not as simple as letting light in through a translucent roof. A roof with a translucency of around 25 per cent will replicate the light levels outside and will provide a minimum of 2,000 lux during daylight hours for 70 per cent of the year, but the problem is that light levels can suddenly change. If, for example, the sun becomes shielded by a cloud, the daylighting outside can suddenly decrease by a factor of ten and the lighting inside will decrease by the same factor. Such a light variation may be acceptable playing cricket outside, but in a contained internal environment with lower light levels, the eye's threshold to accommodate such a change is reduced. In addition, the internal environment has more potential safety hazards with multiple surfaces from which a ball can rebound and the possibility of players of different levels of ability training in close proximity. The solution to this conflict was developed with Max Fordham over a late night teleconference in the run up to the competition deadline. A type of northlight roof was proposed which is engineered to admit sufficient light from only the diffuse part of the sky. The northlight principle was developed to give a more curvilinear S-shaped form, offering better internal reflections and smoothing areas of high contrast to the soffit. The glass line was moved to reduce the surface area of the envelope and create a zone for the internal structure. This development meant that part of the shading element of the roof becomes internal and is not part of the weathering envelope. It was therefore possible to construct this section from a series of sound absorbent fabric louvres, each of which is configured as a miniature northlight.

The design at Lord's scatters light across the underside of the roof to give an overall bright soffit as an ideal backdrop to pick out the small hard red cricket ball without discomfort from glare. The directionality of the daylight also helps give modelling to the ball surface making it easier for batsmen to pick up the subtleties of spin bowling, as if they were outside. This all adds to an uplifting quality which contributes to people's enjoyment of a building. At Lord's this has been achieved in a natural and unaffected way.

Next door to the Indoor School is the office building for the **England and Wales Cricket Board Headquarters**, completed in 1996, which again used the natural daylight strategy as a significant generator of the design. It is a three-storey building and each floor is 15 metres wide. The width was considered deep enough to give good economy and flexibility, but shallow enough to allow for good natural cross-ventilation. In order to also achieve good daylight, the window height was maximised by omitting all suspended ceilings and instead running all of the services in raised floors. This had the added bonus of exposing the thermal mass of the *in situ* concrete floor slabs which helps keep the building cool in summer. Light shelves shade the perimeter offices, that would otherwise be too bright, and bounce daylight into the deep plan office areas. This creates a more even distribution of light and allows the offices to be used without artificial light for much of the day.

The natural light strategy works in harmony with a natural ventilation strategy. There is no glazing below desk level because that would contribute little extra light and would increase potential for solar gain. Instead this space makes a good location for simple perimeter convector heating above which are opening windows to provide natural cross-ventilation.

Designing for natural light does not just inform how buildings are designed but also where they are located. The **Maplethorpe Building** in Oxford, completed in 1999, was the first phase of a development that will allow St Hugh's College to house all of their students on one site. The client's preconception was that the new buildings would follow the pattern of the older buildings around the perimeter of the site, preserving intact the very large central garden. Instead, Morley proposed the buildings in the middle of the site creating a series of gardens that bind together the disparate collection of buildings into a more collegiate whole. This allowed the main residential building to be located on a north-south axis away from any existing trees, so that all study bedrooms face either east or west and benefit from a sunny aspect for half of the day. The Maplethorpe Building comprises study bedrooms on the upper levels where the views, privacy and light are best, with the communal spaces at the base of the building with direct access to the surrounding garden spaces.

OPPOSITE TOP
ECB Headquarters—View from Nursery Ground showing light shelves and glazing above desk height.

OPPOSITE BOTTOM
ECB Headquarters—Storage is in walls at right angles to the window wall and behind the columns to maximise available light—artificial light is an extension of the external light shelf as an up-and-down-lighter to mimic the daylight character.

ABOVE
West elevation of the Maplethorpe Building. Rooms are arranged in clusters of eight per floor around a stair that is expressed externally to break the 96 bedrooms into identifiable social units. The offset tall window, when combined with a handed room gives the appearance of a smaller number of larger windows, helping to reduce the overall scale of the building.

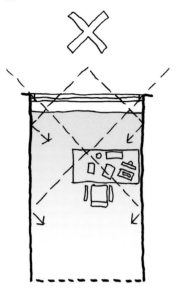

FULLY GLAZED ELEVATION

• Good daylight levels to rear room
• Too bright with glare
• Difficult to set furniture next to window

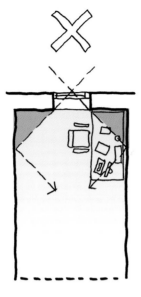

CENTRAL FULLY GLAZED WINDOW

• Dark corners to the room
• Poor light quality—high contrast
• Window prevents desk being located parallel to the window—side light to desk only

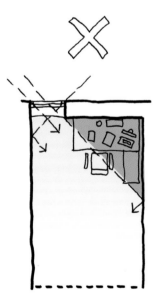

OFFSET FULLY GLAZED WINDOW

• Dark corner to the room
• Poor light quality—high contrast
• No natural light on the desk

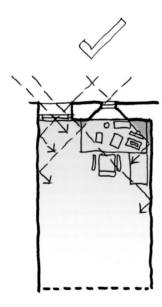

OFFSET FULLY GLAZED WINDOW WITH SIDE WINDOW

• Good light quality—contrast graded across room
• Natural light on the desk
• Minimal dark corners to room

Like the England and Wales Cricket Board Offices, the simple rectangular building form was chosen to be as deep as possible, to be compact and economic. A window wall was then developed to give each study bedroom a good quality of light, with judiciously placed tall windows at the side of each room and small windows above each desk.

Full-height glazing at the base of the building allows the internal social and teaching spaces to flow into the surrounding garden and maximise contact with plants and nature. On the west side the glazing is protected by a green light shelf which provides heavy shade in summer and permits passive solar gain in winter. The interaction between daylight, sunlight and plants has influenced the design from the master plan right the way through to the detail.

LEFT
A variety of options were researched for the window wall—an all glass facade was found to provide too much light and a loss of privacy, a tall central window was found to be good for light penetrating to the back of the room, but gave a high level of contrast between the bright window and the adjacent dark wall. This is resolved by locating the window at the side of the room giving a gently graded wash of light across the adjacent wall. However this option creates a larger dark corner. The proposed solution was to supplement the tall vertical window with a small window just big enough to illuminate the dark corner.

RIGHT
The splayed reveal of the small window is a traditional device to reduce glare and is formed as part of a precast concrete wall panel. The combination of big and small window gives opportunities for fine tuning natural ventilation in winter or summer.

LEFT
Internal view of communal spaces in the
Maplethorpe Building showing how the
green light shelf allows the sun in during the
winter months when more light and warmth
is welcome.

RIGHT
Detail of the west elevation of the Maplethorpe
Building showing how the communal spaces at
the base of the building are shaded to control
the west sun with a green light shelf planted
with white wisteria, giving maximum shade in
summer. Full-height glazing allows the ground
floor spaces to flow into the surrounding garden
and maximise contact with plants and nature.

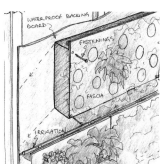

TOP LEFT
David Morley Architects' experimental green wall explores how the cooling effect from plants can be harnessed.

TOP RIGHT
Sketch of student tower proposal for University Partnerships Programme adjacent to Waterloo station.

BOTTOM
Detail of the green wall system installed by Biotecture at David Morley Architects' offices at 18 Hatton Place, London.

Life depends on plants and the integration of plants and architecture is fertile ground for future exploration. It is well established that plants in cities can reduce the heat island effect in cities, they can filter and purify the air, they can reduce the thermal load on buildings, absorb sound, attenuate stormwater and provide a source of food. When placed adjacent to photovoltaic panels they can help keep the panels cool and enhance their efficiency. Green walls, such as the one installed in Morley's offices in 2007, can be made up like a rainscreen cladding system with prefabricated panels clipped to support rails with microbore irrigation which is collected and recycled. The maintenance regime is similar to a window cleaning cycle and, as such, there is the potential to use this technology on extensive areas of buildings. Planting on tall buildings is not a new idea. For example the Torre del Guingi in Lucca has sustained a small garden almost 50 metres in the air for over 500 years. This miniature park provides a welcome cool and shady relief from the hot arid townscape and heralds a theme of lush greenery that forms a linear park which encircles the city along the lines of the original ramparts.

But planting indiscriminately can also destroy our city fabric. For example, in the 1980s a row of plane trees were planted down the centre line of Portland Place. Apart from the Mall, this is one of London's most extensive axial routes. First it was blocked physically by parked cars and now it has been blocked visually by semi-mature trees. As part of a study for the Rifkind Levy Partnership Morley looked at the impact of removing parked cars from some key London streets. In Portland Place it was found that, with a loss of only 30 cars, a new pedestrian route could be created as an extension to the Broad Walk in Regent's Park. This concept has been merged as part of a wider initiative to link the Royal Parks: Regent's Park to the north and St James's Park to the south, in what Sir Terry Farrell has promoted as the "Nash Ramblas". London's Royal Parks demonstrate how plants and nature contribute to making a great city. Indeed the site for Morley's Isis Education Centre in Hyde Park is reported to have the cleanest air in the whole of London.

TOP
Torre del Guingi, Lucca, Italy, fourteenth century.

LEFT
Portland Place, London, showing inappropriate recently planted trees.

RIGHT
Portland Place, as proposed by David Morley Architects.

The **Isis Education Centre**, completed in 2011, is for the ecological and environmental education of children who are being brought up in the city and have had very limited contact with nature. The Royal Parks have a mission to reach many more children than was previously possible. One of the main concerns in designing the building was to translate the notion of fun and what that means in the context of architecture. The built environment is more often a support for fun than fun in itself. Associated with the idea of fun for children are the concepts of refuge, shelter and interaction. On a site with such a high density of trees, the concept of a tree house emerged early on.

The idea of a tree became more of a focus as the design progressed, especially the tree as an archetype of the learning experience referenced by, for example, Issac Newton's apple tree. This was expressed by the architect, design critic and Professor at Yale School of Art and Architecture, Louis I Kahn (1901–1974): "I think of schools as an environment of spaces where it is good to learn. Schools began with a man under a tree, who did not know he was a teacher, discussing his realisation with a few who did not know they were students." That initial concept developed into a building in which the structure is akin to tree trunks and branches, and the roof becomes the canopy for the classrooms. Outside a separate linear block houses the Foundation offices with a glazed foyer connecting the two parts on the axis of the Gatehouse. Service spaces on the other side of the classrooms serve the classrooms indoors and the learning spaces outdoors.

The notion of the building as an interpretation of a tree also makes it into a challenge for children, as it creates a paradox between the familiar and unfamiliar which then hopefully stimulates curiosity. The robust and rustic materials make it attractive yet comfortable enough to touch and interact with. The structure is literally made from tree trunks. French oak timber is used in a form which retains the round cross-section of the tree. The outer rings of a tree trunk are the most structurally efficient part and so this method of using timber, known as timber pole construction, helps to keep the structure light.

OPPOSITE
The Isis Education Centre was conceived as a tree house.

TOP LEFT
The tree as an archetype of the learning experience.

BOTTOM LEFT
The initial concept for the Isis Education Centre developed into a building in which the structure is akin to tree trunks and branches, and the roof becomes its canopy.

RIGHT
The building uses a network of triangulated spars and walls to regularly pick up a heavyweight roof with a lightweight structure.

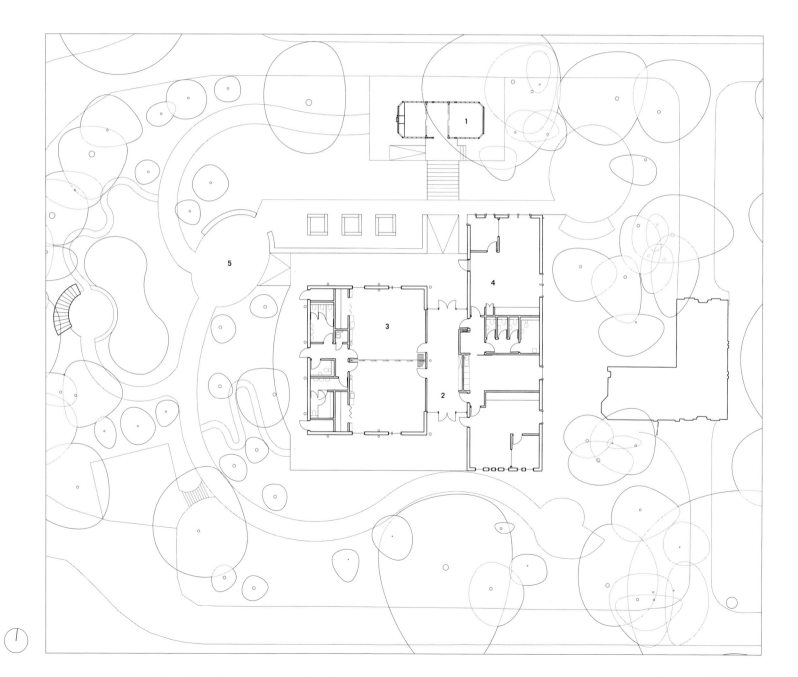

Isis Education Centre Site Plan.
1 Existing gatehouse
2 Entrance foyer
3 Classrooms
4 Offices
5 Outdoor learning zones

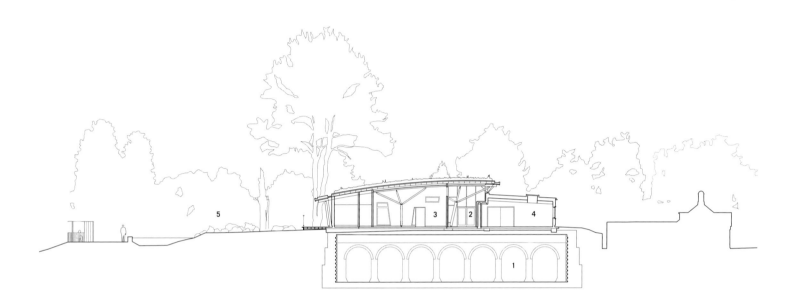

The contact with nature is further emphasised by the brown roof, and timber cladding which blend the building into the landscape, and the pixelated ceiling inspired by the view of the sky through the branches and leaves of a tree. Not seen, but central to maintain the integrity of the concept, the walls and roof of the building have been fully insulated with recycled newspaper. From a brief developed with Dr Nigel Reeve, Head of Ecology for The Royal Parks, the choice of a brown roof was motivated by the aspiration to make as much of the site and the building into a natural habitat, to preserve and enhance the biodiversity of the park. The new building sits on the tarmacadam roof of an old Victorian reservoir and thus transforms an area of no ecological value into a new habitat for the life forms that inhabit Hyde Park.

This project illustrates the design of a building as a "Natural Consequence" of its relationship with nature, but also how buildings have a consequential impact on nature. It is hoped that part of that consequential impact will extend to nurturing an interest amongst the children and adults who visit the centre in society's inter-relationship with all the natural elements. The Victorian reservoir on which the Isis Education Centre is built is a fitting link to the fourth natural element, water.

There are no foundations to the Isis Education Centre since it sits on top of an old Victorian reservoir which will be restored to provide irrigation to Hyde Park.

1 Victorian reservoir
2 Entrance foyer
3 Classrooms
4 Offices
5 Outdoor learning zones

TOP
Stainless steel connections create strong pin joints that direct the loads straight along the outer rings of the timber—making the most of their structural ability.

BOTTOM
The new landscape at the Isis Education Centre respects the mature trees and bushes on the site with a nature walkway, incorporating opportunities for butterfly gardens, sensory areas, shrubberies, den-making and pond dipping, encouraging children to explore and experience a range of habitats supporting many different kinds of wildlife from birds to bugs.

OPPOSITE
The contact with nature is further emphasised by the brown roof, and timber cladding which blend the building into the landscape. The wall structures use Orientated Strand Board panels which are made from bonded chips of wood waste rather than peeled logs, so trees are integrated into this building from concept to finer detail.

OPPOSITE
Water Polo Venue for London 2012
Olympic Games

LEFT
View from the Olympic Stadium towards
the Water Polo Venue on the left and the
Aquatics Centre on the righ

Water is a significant generator of architectural form. In the most rudimentary sense buildings protect from the harmful effects of water whether it be falling from the sky, percolating through the earth or permeating through the air as moisture. Water is also an increasingly precious resource which can be nurtured through good design whether it be water appliances that make water feel wetter and thus reduce consumption or roofs that allow rainwater to be recycled for irrigation or WC flushing. Water can be a source of immense pleasure and the following examples show the natural consequences of responding to its many facets.

The temporary 5,000 seat Water Polo Venue for the London 2012 Olympic Games is conceived as a kit of parts. Some of the components are pre-cycled, coming from the existing supply chain for temporary structures. Virtually all of the components will return and replenish the supply chain after the games. Huge temporary structures are most readily constructed using a re-deployable fabric envelope. For London 2012 it became possible to introduce new phthalate free forms of PVC which can be folded up and reused without creasing but can also be recycled in a closed loop manufacturing process at the end of their re-use life. However, water sports require a more sophisticated enclosure to prevent problems with condensation arising from the high moisture levels around swimming pools and this has had a critical influence on the design of this venue.

The "5-D Geometry" chapter will describe how the cross-section was evolved from optimising sightlines and public circulation by placing the majority of the seats opposite the referees' platform, where there are less obstructed views. It is noted that the seating tiers, which are off the shelf components, just happen to be 500 millimetres high and 800

Cross-section through the Water Polo Venue.
1 Entrance concourse
2 Main stand
3 Competition pool
4 VIP stand
5 Warm-up pool

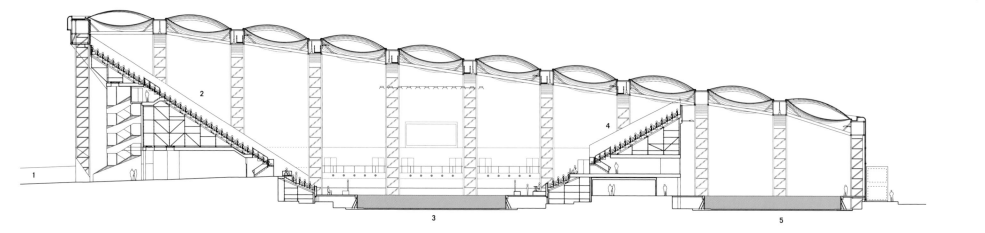

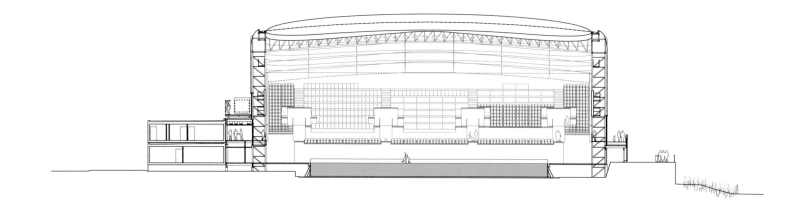

millimetres deep—the golden section. But this section could equally be described as a consequence of the environmental control strategy. The condensation risk is reduced by constructing the roof from a double-membrane which is inflated to form huge 50 by ten metre wide air cushions that provide sufficient insulation as well as making them self supporting between the lighting gantries. The asymmetric shape allows a mechanically conditioned air bubble to be created above the competition pool and allows the form of the building to promote natural ventilation of the main stand—air is drawn in below the seats and rises out through its natural buoyancy to be extracted through louvres at high level.

The "Natural Consequence" of this building is that there are many reasons for its distinctive shape. It has to do with the way the inside works for the sightlines and environmental controls, in harmony with a view of how the building worked from the outside. From the outside it combines with the adjacent venues to form two triumvirates. The first is the group of three adjacent venues at the centre of the Olympic Park: the Olympic Stadium, the Aquatics Centre and Water Polo. The second is the group of three temporary structures that define the zone of the Olympic Park devoted to water sports comprising Water Polo and the two temporary wings to the Aquatics Centre, which combine together to create what is known as the Water Park.

At the entrance to the Olympic Park the profile of the Water Polo Venue allows a vista to unfold of the Olympic Stadium. The rippling wave forms of the roof cushions are analogous to a huge splash created by the diving figure represented by the Aquatics Centre.

OPPOSITE
Outdoor Pool at The Hurlingham Club in West London.

LEFT
View of the model showing the site context. The ornamental lake is at the top, tennis courts to the left, the River Thames below and the new pool surrounded by sunbathing areas and the new pavilion are on the right.

On a smaller scale, the **Outdoor Pool at The Hurlingham Club** in West London, completed in 2011, can also be seen as the "Natural Consequence" of the brief and the historical context. The original outdoor pool facilities were 80 years old and, though much loved by the members for their character and charm, they had reached the end of their design life. The resulting scheme comprises a 30 metre long pool, a children's pool and beach area, a changing room building and a cafe, integrated into the picturesque landscaped grounds of the Club which abuts the Hurlingham Park and River Thames in Fulham. The new buildings draw on the rhythm, scale and materials of the originals, including adopting the distinctive Club colours, while providing modern standards of accommodation and a facility for the members to enjoy for the next 80 years. The swimming pool area has been long established and many people were sensitive to the changes. However, feedback from members following the completion of the new pool is that the new facilities have solved the practical problems of the old facilities without losing their character.

The 80 year old facility had several technical problems around the pools and the often cramped changing area was no longer fit for purpose. The Club was founded in 1867 as "an agreeable country resort" and its picturesque grounds were originally conceived as a countrified landscape in the tradition of the English country garden. The site retains the location of the original pool built in 1933, which itself occupied the site of a former sluice connecting the ornamental lake to the north with the River Thames to the south.

TOP

The rhythm of white louvred doors was emphasised by creating in and out doors to each changing room space: male, female and family. The clerestory glass is set back allowing reflected light from the pool to light up the timber stressed skin structure.

BOTTOM

The old pavilion was considered by the Members to be an evocative backdrop for swimming as an almost theatrical event. However the site had mechanical problems. The low water level meant you could not appreciate the landscape whilst swimming, there were unsightly pool covers and the entrance at the middle split the pavilion in two and created crowding at the poolside.

The planning of the buildings and ancillary pools was designed to maximise the useable space but also blur the boundaries between the pool compound and its surrounding landscape. The existing changing pavilion was an awkwardly thin building along the west side of the pool and although the new pavilion is in the same location it pushes right out to follow the curved alignment of the adjacent pathways in order to integrate this fairly large building into the landscape. The curved plan extending to maximum limits allows space to flow around the building anchoring the curvilinear form of the lake and creating a prow which viewed across the water would appear on the scale of a gazebo in the landscape. The roof is lifted clear of the changing room facade allowing daylight, and sunlight reflected from the water, to permeate the internal spaces, also giving views from within to the tree canopies and the grounds beyond.

The Hurlingham Outdoor Pool can be seen as a "Natural Consequence" of practical considerations of environmental control (the building is naturally ventilated and naturally lit during daylight hours), effective spatial organisation and the management of water for leisure, cleansing and for all its visual attributes. However it also illustrates a natural response to peoples' emotions and to an historical context. This began with going back to first principles to identify what members liked about the original building, in effect, identifying the 'DNA' of the site.

TOP
The blue theme is kept for the inside. Outside, the pavilion looks like a planted garden wall providing a backdrop to the adjacent tennis courts. The roof is articulated in scale to relate to the surrounding landscape and resembles a series of five upturned boats floating above the garden wall.

BOTTOM
The modular arrangement of changing rooms and shower blocks follows the rhythm of the roof above and suggests the appearance inside of sheltering under an upturned boat. The rippling effects of the water can be seen on the soffit.

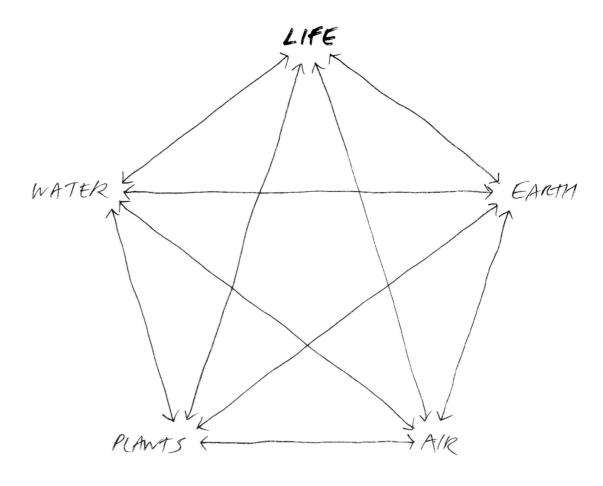

The projects shown in this chapter illustrate designs influenced by four elements of nature: earth, air, plants and water. It becomes apparent that none of the natural elements work in isolation, they are all interrelated. The example of the tree shows an organic structure derived as a natural consequence of a balanced relationship between the earth, air or light, plants and water. The analogy of the tree and architecture can be taken further. A tree is part of an eco-system upon which the health of the planet depends. That eco-system is currently being stressed by the needs of society. Likewise a work of architecture responds not just to the needs of an individual client, but to society as a whole. This brings a fifth natural element into play.

It is commonly held in many cultures that there are five natural elements, albeit no consensus as to what the fifth element is.[1] For the purposes of understanding what is meant by "Natural Consequences" the fifth element can be considered here as the product of DNA, the life itself from which society has evolved. For all the projects shown in this chapter, the specific response to nature has been a product of the particular needs of society applying to that project.

From an environmental point of view, there is an urgent need for these five elements—earth, air, plants, water and society to have a balanced relationship. This applies to the design of buildings and cities as much as it does to the life of trees. When these five elements are in harmony, architecture should also be natural and unaffected. Architecture will occur as a "Natural Consequence" when the fifth natural element, life, works in harmony with the other four, earth, air, plants and water.

The next chapter, "5-D Geometry" expands on the nature of such harmonious relationships.

1. According to Keith Critchlow in *The Hidden Geometry of Flowers* "The sages of earlier human societies taught that 'nature' was the great educator. The Chinese Master Chu Tzu or Chu His (AD 1130-1200) says in his commentary on Yang and Yin, the two most fundamental universal forces: The teachings concerning Yang and Yin and the five elements (or agents of materiality) are made visible in the book of Nature so that humanity may learn.

OPPOSITE
The new facilities have retained a sense of the theatrical setting for swimming.

ABOVE
The five natural elements according to "Five by 5".

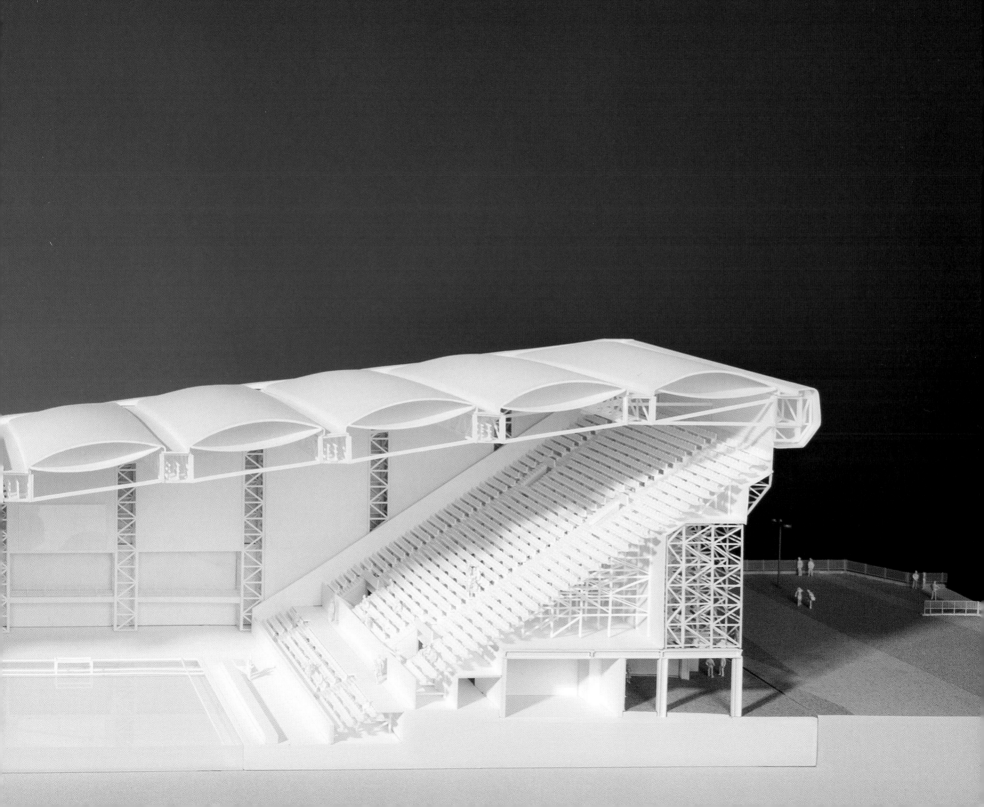

Not to get too mystical about this, but architects have always had a thing about geometry and the way it can describe natural form. Snail shells, pine cones, the consequences of relationships between consenting rabbits, all manner of things have a form that might be expressed in a mathematical sequence, such as the Fibonacci series (named after Leonardo Pisano Bigollo of Pisa, a mathematician, known as Leonardo Fibonacci). Fibonacci numbers are produced from the sum of the two preceding numbers, starting with 0, and 1. Its rhythms are found frequently in nature and the study of architecture in plants is called phyllotaxy. Another Leonardo—Da Vinci—was the first to suggest that the adaptive advantage of the Fibonacci pattern in plants is to maximise exposure to dew. Today's naturalists agree. Phyllotactic architecture in plants optimises access to moisture, rainfall and sunlight.

So does capturing the numerical relationships in the geometry of architecture confer a 'natural' legitimacy on a manufactured aesthetic? Should architects design with an arithmetical answer in mind because it will produce the 'right' answer?

The quest for a source of harmony and rhythm in form has frequently reverted to mathematics as a way of helping explain where observable, sensual harmony might reside. If the apprehension of it is a physiological reaction, then it is understandable we should seek to explain it, and reproduce its benefits—like a good flint arrowhead, the front of the Parthenon, or indeed a Jean Muir dress.

In which dimension might the sensation of taking pleasure from architecture exist? Why not the 'fifth'? It's as good a place as any if you consider the preceding four have pretty much been occupied. Let's claim the fifth for our physiological response to perceived harmony and delight. And before we get too comfy in the fifth, it would be churlish to deny our pleasurable response to the non-geometrical, chaotic and inharmonious ("God Save the Queen" by the Sex Pistols perhaps, or something a bit random by a confirmed parametricist).

However, where geometry is at work, it is a proven tool for measuring the relationship between architecture and nature that lends our understanding greater precision. David Morley Architects has frequently found serendipitous harmony in and around the number five, or multiples of it, sitting as it does at a significant point early in the Fibonacci series (not too small, not too big), and allowing for simple easy symmetries around its central digit.

Other geometries are also at work in DMA's work, so for example the gently sloping wedge of the Water Polo Arenas's roof in the Olympic Park is set up by two different seating rakes established by the asymmetrical location of the judges' seat at one side of the pool. The soft twists of silver roof extensions (five per wing) on Urban Splash's Velvet Mill in Bradford create a harmonious, vibrant contrast with the listed mill below, and allow for a double-height which a more orthogonal approach would not have achieved without eroding the pristine geometry of the original. The five bays in Lord's Cricket School, its innovative northlights, and its net lanes that are no longer perpendicular to the roof openings, but parallel to allow the ball to travel through unbanded light—all these geometries, help explain—rather than determine—why some buildings work. Geometry is an optional tool that accelerates us towards solutions that help create the most valuable dimension of architectural pleasure—the fifth.

LEE MALLETT

PREVIOUS PAGES
Model of the London 2012 Water Polo Arena showing the asymmetric cross-section generated by the spectator sight lines.

OPPOSITE
View of one of the eight nets at the Lord's Indoor Cricket School showing the geometry of the rooflights which cut out any distraction from direct sunlight.

Geometry brings precision and accuracy to the relationship between nature and architecture. It offers the potential for certainty in an apparently chaotic environment. Through an understanding of the mathematical structures found in nature, there is the potential for the application of geometry to go beyond purely functional arrangements to a more fundamental level of defining the spirit of a place. The concept of 5-D geometry emerged from an examination of 25 years of David Morley Architects' work and the unexplained fact that so many of the practice's buildings are easily sub-divisible into units of five. This chapter explores why that should be and how five dimensions of geometry can be deployed in the design process. Geometry is commonly thought of in either two or three dimensions but

three other dimensions can also be considered giving one-, four- and five-dimensional geometry.

1-D Geometry conveys information without describing shape. This is the best way to start a project, with an open mind. It also describes modules and rhythms.

2-D Geometry describes areas without volume. This allows space planning arrangements to be explored, adjacencies to be tested and the capacity of a site to accommodate a building footprint to be analysed. 2-D analysis means parameters can be established so the design process can commence.

5'END

3'END

3'END

5'END

3'END

$R = 93\,M\ MILES$

● MEAN OF EARTH + VENUS ORBIT

EARTH : R = 93 MILLION MILES
ORBIT = 365.3 DAYS

VENUS : R = 67 MILLION MILES
ORBIT = 224.7 DAYS

$$\frac{365.3}{224.7} \approx \frac{8}{5} \approx \phi$$

3-D Geometry is where design begins and spaces and volumes can be explored. There are many tools available, ranging from the freehand sketch to three-dimensional computer-based Building Information Modelling systems. 3-D Geometry allows optioneering and evaluation.

It is widely held that the fourth dimension of space is time. Time affects architecture in many ways from establishing an historical context, defining periods of change, the dynamics of sound and the ever-changing environmental conditions. 4-D Geometry is when a design solution comes alive through its relationship with the natural elements, movement, sound and light.

But there is more to geometry than that. Geometric structures can be observed from the tiniest to the most immense manifestations of nature—from DNA molecules to the trajectory of the planet Venus. There is therefore scope to explore how geometry effects human emotions and spirit in the broadest possible sense. This is what is considered here as the fifth dimension of geometry. The relevance of five is in part because it is a natural progression, one step beyond four dimensions, but also because the number five itself has a special significance in allowing harmonious relationships to be created. The following examples of the practice's work illustrate how these five dimensions of geometry can be deployed.

LEFT
The helical structure of DNA molecules.

RIGHT
The mean of the combined trajectory of the orbits of Earth and Venus around the Sun.

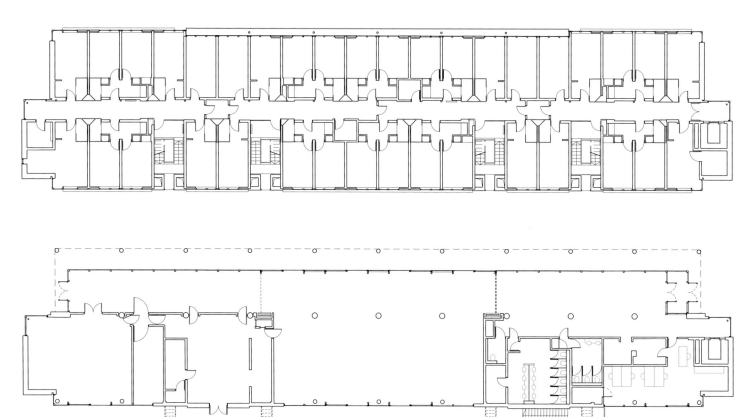

TOP
Third floor plan of the Maplethorpe Building showing the arrangement of four number eight bedroom flats which, with the additional modules for a pantry and stair, give a sub-division of five bays on each elevation.

BOTTOM
Ground floor plan of the Maplethorpe Building showing the sub-division of ten structural bays into five pairs.

OPPOSITE
Master plan for St Hugh's College showing proposed new buildings in grey. The first phase, the Maplethorpe Building, is a linear building which, when combined with an avenue of existing beech trees, defines a new formal garden at the centre of the college.

First, the **Maplethorpe Building** at St Hugh's College in Oxford shows the benefits of beginning a project in one dimension. Morley's initial competition-winning approach to get selected was to talk about the importance of dialogue and communication in creating the best solution to meet the College's needs. By contrast, the competing architects presented only designs, none of which found favour with the Governing Body of the College.

A breakthrough in the concept for planning the College also came from the one-dimensional geometry of the written word. The Maplethorpe Building was the first phase of a development that has allowed St Hugh's College to house all of their students on site. The Governing Body recognised the need to begin with a master plan, since their site occupied an entire city block, which had been acquired incrementally over time and had never been comprehensively planned. Their preconception was that the new buildings would follow the pattern of the older buildings around the perimeter of the site, preserving intact the very large central garden. The idea for a new master plan came from a quote from the inspirational academic, theorist and architectural critic Colin Rowe (1920–1999). In his review of the competition entries for Churchill College in Cambridge, published in the *The Architectural Review*, he said that "the one thing that all the architects agreed on was that a College implied a courtyard and that the more courtyards a College possessed, the more Collegiate it would become".

This inspired a controversial proposal for St Hugh's, which was renowned for its generous historic garden. The concept was to build right in the middle of the garden and use the new buildings to define a sequence of smaller gardens, which would help to define a more collegiate infrastructure. Since the design strategy was initially formulated in words, without drawings, this can be considered as deploying one-dimensional geometry.

The St Hugh's master plan was developed further to allow the new buildings to benefit from daylight and sunlight. The student rooms are arranged on a north–south axis away from any existing trees, so that all study bedrooms face either east or west and benefit from a sunny aspect for half of the day. The Maplethorpe Building formed the first phase of development. It is a simple four-storey rectangular building which comprises study bedrooms on the three upper levels where the views, privacy and light are best, with the communal spaces at the base of the building with direct access to the surrounding garden. The scale of the building is broken down hierarchically to reflect its social organisation. In Oxford, student rooms were traditionally planned around a staircase, which became a social unit, commonly comprising eight rooms. The Maplethorpe Building houses 96 rooms in total, served by four stairs each serving 24 rooms arranged in clusters of eight rooms per floor. It is a modular structure and each eight room cluster includes two additional

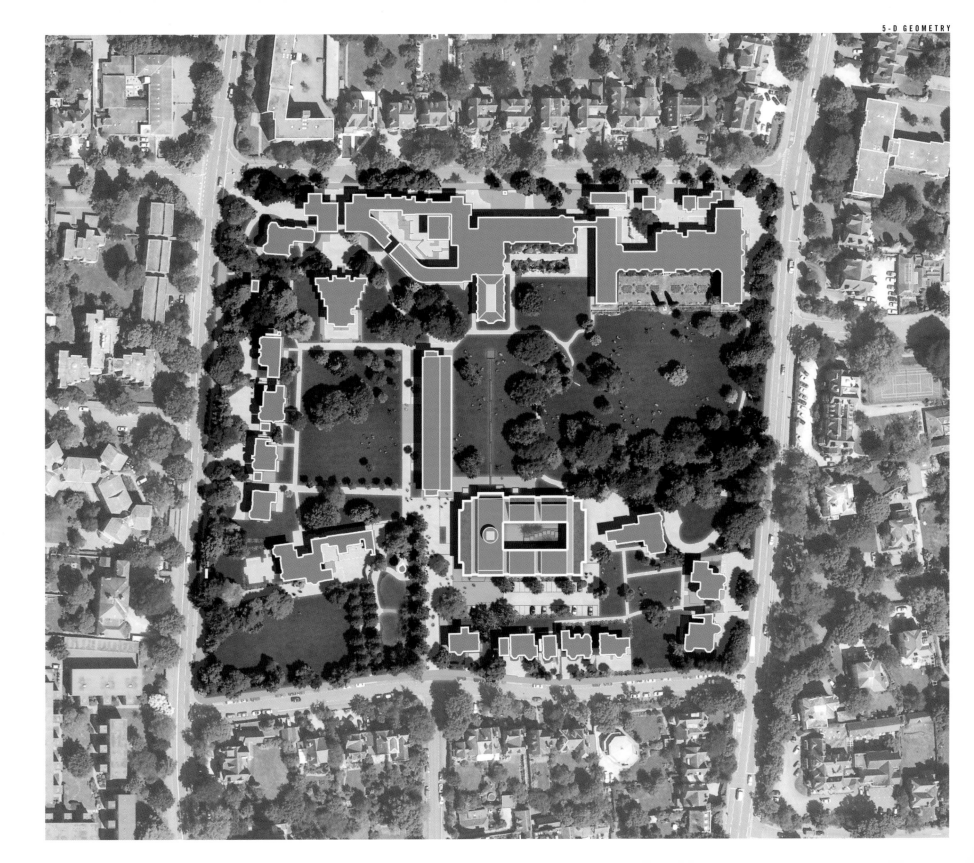

RIGHT
East elevation of the Maplethorpe Building
showing the ten bay colonnade and the six
bay logia.

OPPOSITE TOP
One-dimensional geometry defines repetitive
sequences and rhythms such as that
generated by Fibonacci numbers.

OPPOSITE BOTTOM
Detail of the east elevation showing the
division into eight terracotta tiles.

modules, one for a pantry and one for the stair, giving ten modules per cluster arranged as five modules each side of a central corridor. To give future flexibility the structure spans across two bedroom modules so that on each facade there are ten structural bays. The residential entrances are all from the west garden via boldly expressed staircases, which emphasise the social groupings. The east elevation faces towards a new garden which has been created at the centre of the College and is given a more communal character. The ground floor is set back to create a covered colonnade which links together the north and south parts of the College. On the upper level,

six of the ten structural bays are set back to create the character of a logia overlooking the central garden. This creates a rhythm of ten to six, or five to three. The hierarchy of scale extends beyond the bedroom module to the cladding components where the panels between windows are divided into eight large format terracotta tiles. The combination of elements into groups of 1, 2, 3, 5 and 8 illustrates a second example of 1-D Geometry whereby a sequence of units can be manipulated to create a rhythm. The particular sequence shown here is notable because it forms the beginning of a Fibonacci sequence.[1]

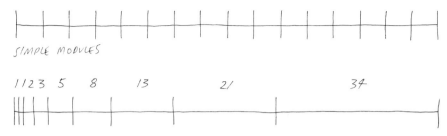

SIMPLE MODULES

1 1 2 3 5   8   13   21   34

FIBONACCI RATIOS

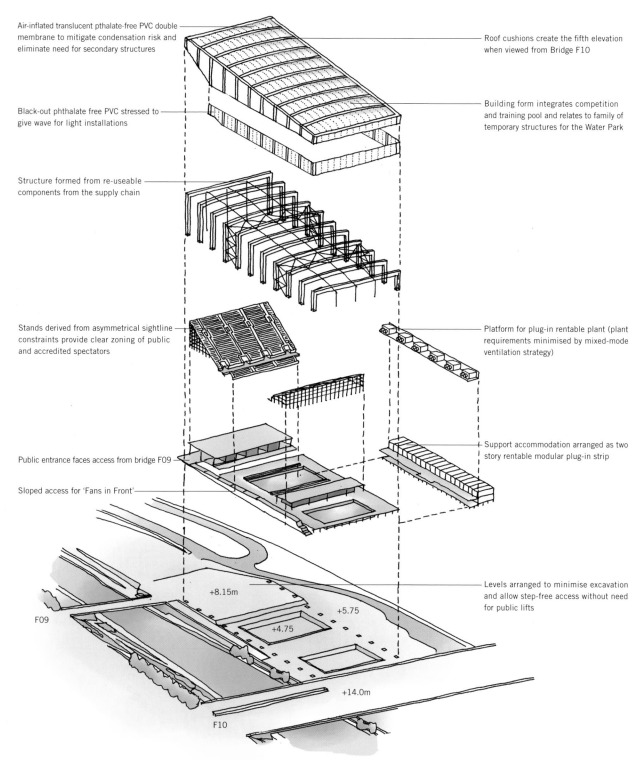

Air-inflated translucent pthalate-free PVC double membrane to mitigate condensation risk and eliminate need for secondary structures

Black-out phthalate free PVC stressed to give wave for light installations

Structure formed from re-useable components from the supply chain

Stands derived from asymmetrical sightline constraints provide clear zoning of public and accredited spectators

Public entrance faces access from bridge F09

Sloped access for 'Fans in Front'

Roof cushions create the fifth elevation when viewed from Bridge F10

Building form integrates competition and training pool and relates to family of temporary structures for the Water Park

Platform for plug-in rentable plant (plant requirements minimised by mixed-mode ventilation strategy)

Support accommodation arranged as two story rentable modular plug-in strip

Levels arranged to minimise excavation and allow step-free access without need for public lifts

+8.15m

+5.75

+4.75

+14.0m

F09

F10

Diagram of the 'kit of parts' from which the Water Polo Arena can be constructed and de-constructed.

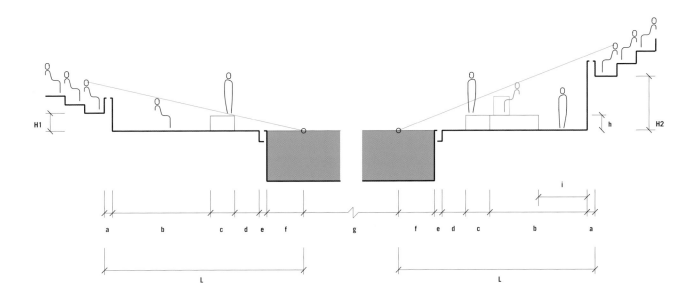

H1

H2

h

a b c d e f g f e d c b a

i

L L

2-D Geometry is a well-established part of architectural design and enables the parameters of a project to be explicitly defined. This is particularly the case when designing for sport, where each sport can impose precise dimensional constraints on architecture. This applies as much to the plan as the cross-section and, in many respects, it is the cross-section which begins to define the character of a sports building. For example the cross-section of Morley's design for the temporary **Water Polo Arena** for the London 2012 Olympic Games was derived from a 2-D analysis. There was no budget for iconic structures and the Water Polo Arena design had to be driven by a creative approach to achieving cost effectiveness and build-ability. However, the site was one of the most prominent of the Olympic Park and the design team sought an integrated solution that would respond to the challenge to deliver cost effectively an amazing arena for sport that would also befit the prominent site. The concept was driven by the desire to make the building from a 'kit of parts', where all of the components can be efficiently re-used or re-cycled. Indeed many components were pre-cycled taken from the existing supply chain. This was the first bespoke Water Polo Arena ever built for an Olympic Games, presenting an opportunity to evolve

from first principles an appropriate building form which achieves the best balance between the internal 2-D geometric constraints provided by the brief, and a response to the external site conditions.

For watching Water Polo, spectators want to be as close to the action as possible. Although some athletes prefer to be surrounded by spectators on all four sides, the views from the sides are better than views from behind the goals. With a capacity of 5,000 a fantastic venue can be achievable with spectators on just two sides. However, on one side the sightlines are complicated by a continuous elevated row of desks for the referees. In order to address these issues, the spectators are distributed asymmetrically with a large stand for the public and a smaller stand for the accredited spectators. Atmosphere is retained on both sides of the pools by ensuring that the front four rows of seats of the accredited stand are allocated to general spectators.

This arrangement allowed excellent C90 sightlines to be achieved with standard off the peg seating systems.[2] The sightline geometry is determined initially by the relationship between the edge of the 'field of play' and the

Criteria for sightlines in a water polo venue showing the different constraints on each side of the pool.

H1 Determined by referee's cat walk
H2 Determined by official's head height
L a+b+c+d+e+f=8.14 metres
a Airblade
b Walkway
c Referee's cat walk
d Set back from pool edge
e Gutter
f Width to 'field of play'
g 20 metre
h Referee's cat walk height
i Official's desk platform

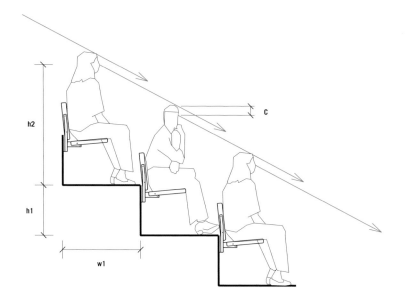

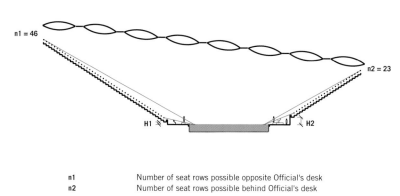

n1 = 46

n2 = 23

H1   H2

| n1 | Number of seat rows possible opposite Official's desk |
| n2 | Number of seat rows possible behind Official's desk |

$$\text{where } n1 = \frac{h1(L+w1) - C(L+w1) - w1(H1+h2)}{C1 \times w1} \text{ and } n2 = \frac{h1(L+w1) - C(L+w1) - w1(H2 + h2)}{C1 \times w1}$$

LEFT
Geometry of C90 sightlines.
C   'C' Value = 90 millimetres
h1   Riser height = 0.5 metres
h2   Assumed eye height = 1.2 metres
w1   Riser depth = 0.8 metres

RIGHT
Cross-section through the Water Polo Arena
showing sightlines.

OPPOSITE
The geometry of the cross-section is strongly
expressed on the side elevations.

distance and elevation of the front row of seats. With a straight slope of seating the sightlines get progressively worse for spectators the higher up the slope they are. This can be compensated for by making the seating progressively steeper either in increments, as for example at the Olympic Stadium where there are three sections of seating each set at a slightly steeper angle, or by arranging the seats in a continuous parabolic curve, such as found in Greek theatres such as Ephesus. There is a maximum steepness determined by UK safety legislation of 35 degrees. For Water Polo it was necessary to find a kit of parts for the seating, which could be widely used elsewhere. A standard seating rake of 0.8 metre deep platforms by 0.5 metre high risers fell within the steepness parameter and was found to accommodate a variety of off the shelf seating systems. The cross-section for the building was then generated by defining the lowest possible location for the front row of seats behind the referees' desks whereby spectators could see over the referees' heads and projecting from that point backwards a 0.8 by 0.5 metre rake of seats as far as possible until the C90 sightlines were compromised. This gave 23 rows.

Then, on the opposite side of the pool, the same exercise was applied, this time from a lower starting position which was also slightly closer to the pool edge since there are no referees' desks. This gave 46 rows, generating the precise geometry of the asymmetric cross-section.

Geometry is there to support a building concept and the asymmetric bowl also achieved other objectives. It generates a sloping roof, which can be extended beyond the lower stand to create a smaller enclosure for the warm up pool. It makes the public stand as high as possible in such a way that creates a natural sign towards the entrance. It works for the environmental control, as described in "Natural Consequences", and it works for the context.

Although not a legacy building the Water Polo Venue held a key position, albeit the junior member, in a triumvirate with the legacy Olympic Stadium and the legacy Aquatics Centre. It was proposed that Water Polo

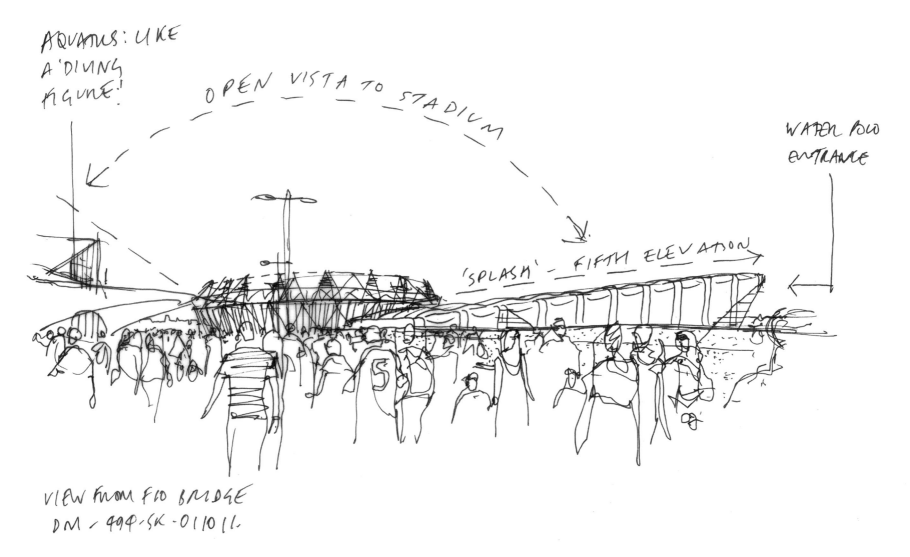

AQUATICS: LIKE A 'DIVING FIGURE'!

OPEN VISTA TO STADIUM

WATER POLO ENTRANCE

'SPLASH' - FIFTH ELEVATION

VIEW FROM FOO BRIDGE
DM - 499 - SK - 011011.

acknowledged this relationship in particular with the adjacent Aquatics Centre. This was especially in terms of views on entering the site where Aquatics and Water Polo framed the view and set the scene for the entrance, approach, arrival sequence culminating in the Olympic Stadium, and in the reverse views from the Stadium where the two buildings acted as a backdrop. The proposed venue has a distinctive form that complements the curvilinear lines of the Aquatics Centre with a gently rippling roof that could be seen as the splash generated by the diving form of the Aquatics Building. The low profile of the venue adjacent to the main entrance bridge gives the appearance of a structure growing out from under the bridge and responds sympathetically with the projecting prow of the Aquatics Centre above the bridge. The massing when viewed from the bridge is completely subservient to and complementary to the unveiled vista of the Main Stadium. When viewed from the Olympic Park, the massing has the benefit of naturally creating a focus on the entrance to

the Water Polo Arena, which is from a smaller adjacent pedestrian bridge. It was also noted that the legacy Aquatics Centre during the Games, was dominated by its temporary side extensions. A second triumvirate was therefore proposed where the Water Polo Arena became the senior member of a suite of temporary structures that grew out from the Aquatics Legacy Building and combined together to define a Water Park. The temporary nature of these buildings made it logical that they should be complementary in their architectural language. It was proposed that, being the senior member of this group of temporary structures in the Water Park, the Water Polo Arena had a refined and distinctive quality derived from the theme of water and an innovative approach to new levels of sustainability and re-use. In terms of building silhouette and height, there seemed good opportunities to control the visual expression of the venue and strengthen the drama and scale of the approach, allowing the two building silhouettes to communicate without other clutter.

OPPOSITE
View from the most distant seat showing the high quality of the sightlines.

ABOVE
Sketch view of the main approach to the Olympic Park.

RIGHT
The design and fabrication of the Velvet
Mill penthouses deployed the same 3-D
computer parametric modelling software.

OPPOSITE
Sketch view showing Velvet Mill in the
context of the master plan for Lister Mills.

The side elevations are a simple expression of the 2-D cross-section reinforcing the dynamic shape of the competition bowl. A point for future reference is the particular angle of the seating tiers generated by the best fitting standard seating systems on the market. The standard 0.5 metre high by 0.8 metre deep platforms are in the ratio of five to eight which approximates to the golden ratio.[3] The seating bowl is therefore an expression of what could be called the "golden angle". A further point of reference is the rhythm of structural bays resulting from dividing the overall 122 metre length of the venue by the optimum spans of the inflated air cushion roof combined with the width of the structural frames. This gave 11 rows of two metre wide frames defining ten rows of ten metre wide structural bays. This is the same number of structural bays as found at the Maplethorpe Building and also as adopted for the **Velvet Mill** project that features in "Evolution vs Revolution".

The revolutionary aspect of the roof of Velvet Mill is that it was conceived and fabricated using 3-D computer software that didn't exist before the twenty-first century. There was a seamless progression in the design process working with engineer Tim Lucas of Price and Myers 3-D Engineering, from initial form development with their Solid Works software through to them feeding detailed cutting patterns directly to the computer, with numerically controlled cutting machines in the workshops using the same software. Neither the design of the Velvet Mill penthouses, nor the fabrication could have been accomplished using 2-D geometry alone.

Notwithstanding that, the parameters of the 3-D model were based on a 2-D overlay of a circular weaving pattern generated from the module of the original Dennett's arches. To achieve a comfortable fit it transpired that the diameter of each circle equated to five modules of the original structure

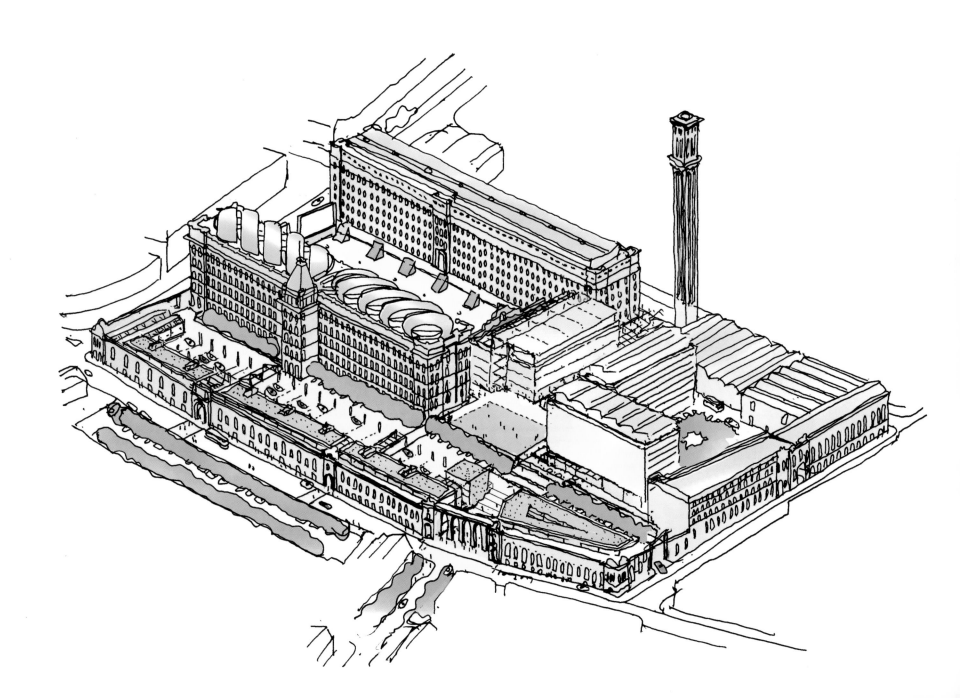

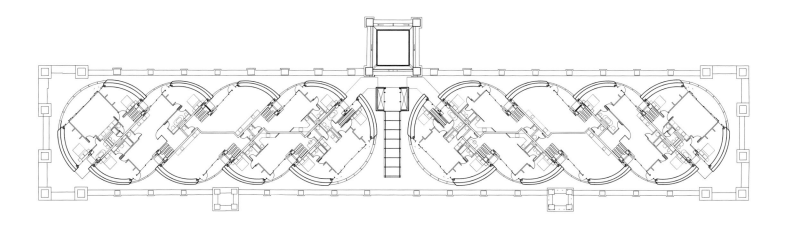

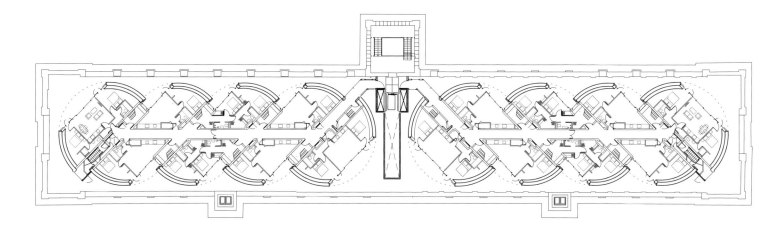

TOP
Upper level penthouses plan.

BOTTOM
Lower level penthouses plan.

and the circular pattern could be repeated five times on each side of the building, giving ten bays overall. This illustrates the inter-dependencies of the geometric dimensions: a concept that can be described in words (1-D), a linear sequence of five repeated modules (1-D), a base pattern of intersecting circles (2-D) and a curvilinear plait generated from that pattern and constructed in 3-D.

So-called "3-D parametric modelling" has liberated the mass production of complex organic forms in architecture which previously could only be hand-crafted. At Velvet Mill, the form generating software was used to produce shapes which would not only have been difficult to make, but also difficult to imagine. The power of parametric modelling can be taken much further as a tool to generate designs, but there needs to be a balance between the extraordinary and the familiar to ensure that there

is still a place for the extraordinary. This is explored further in "Evolution vs Revolution". At Velvet Mill, 3-D engineering was used as a tool to bring new life to a handsome old structure and not to fudge the difference between old with the new, each part has its own integrity and all parts are in harmony respecting similar ambitions, the structural grain and using appropriate technologies.

4-D geometry introduces the dimension of time and movement. The movement of the sun and earth over time has particular significance for architecture. For many building types it is possible to ensure that the majority of spaces are naturally lit for much of the year and this is a means to both save energy and create places that people enjoy. The success of a daylight strategy will depend on the extent to which the benefits of natural light can be obtained without being compromised by solar gain or glare from the sun.

LEFT
Relationship of new structure to existing
Dennett's arches below.

TOP RIGHT
Concept development using Solid Works
software.

MIDDLE RIGHT
2-D circular plan geometry from which 3-D
forms were generated.

BOTTOM RIGHT
Inspiration from the tradition of weaving in
the building.

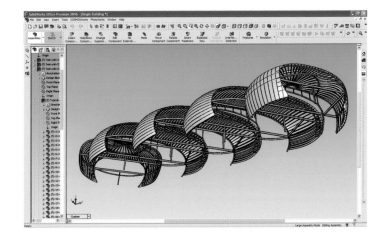

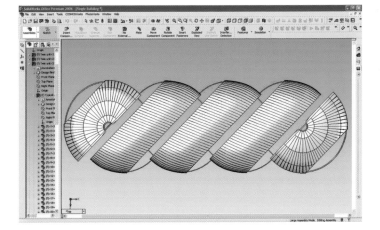

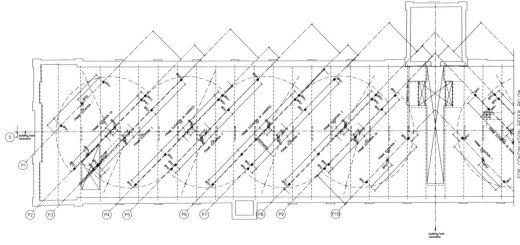

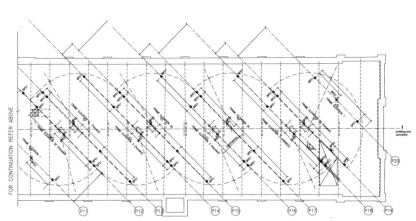

LEFT
Computer-generated view from ground level
of the proposed penthouses.

TOP RIGHT
Roof structure under manufacture with
cutting machines using the Solid Works
software model.

BOTTOM RIGHT
3-D double curvature roof panels being
hoisted to roof level.

View of the re-furbished ground level
community space showing the retained
Dennett's arches.

RIGHT
The main entrance to the Lord's Indoor
Cricket School faces northeast, therefore the
glazed areas do not require shading from
the sun.

This was especially the case in the design of the **Lord's Indoor Cricket School** featured in "Natural Consequences". The movement of the sun was carefully studied in relation to the orientation of the site, to see if glazed areas could be designed to face only the diffuse part of the sky where there is no direct sunlight during the hours of operation. This was necessary both to avoid solar gain but also to eliminate the sudden changes of lighting levels that occur when the sun is concealed behind a passing cloud. Initially a northlight solution was explored but this did not suit the orientation of the site which is on a southwest to northeast axis. However, a northlight solution is effective in blocking the sun between six o'clock in the morning to six o'clock in the evening whereas the Cricket School operating hours are normally between 9.30 am to 10.30 pm and so a northlight would not block out the later evening sun. The solution was therefore to orientate the rooflights to the northeast, which both blocked out the sun during the critical hours of operation and suited the orientation of the site.

The concept for the barrel vaulted 'S' shaped rooflights is explained in "Natural Consequences" but the precise geometry was determined by the movement of the sun and the quantity of light required. A daylight factor of 25 per cent was proposed and, as a rule of thumb, this gave a required aspect ratio for the height to width of each rooflight of one to four. However, to allow for the obstructions caused by structure and glazing frames, an aspect ratio of one to three was targeted. Each barrel vault was designed to cover two 3.6 metre wide nets giving an overall width for each vault of 7.2 metres defining a necessary height of 2.4 metres (one third of 7.2 metres). Within that height it became possible to incorporate a deep truss, which could efficiently span along the length of the building. The integration of the primary structure with the rooflights eliminated the need for any secondary support structures for the cricket nets and artificial lights. The thickness of the bottom chords of the trusses, together with the width of the artificial lights and an area of translucent film on the roof

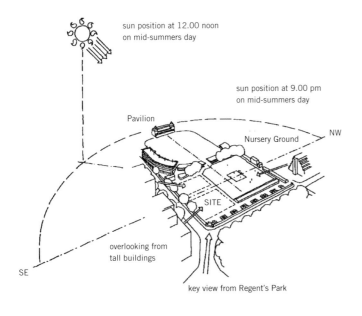

sun position at 12.00 noon
on mid-summers day

sun position at 9.00 pm
on mid-summers day

Pavilion

Nursery Ground

NW

SITE

overlooking from
tall buildings

SE

key view from Regent's Park

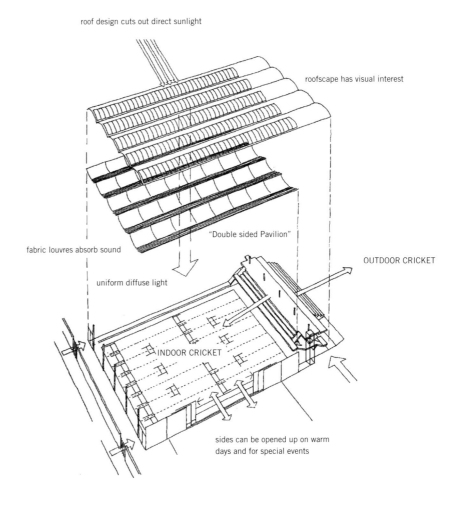

roof design cuts out direct sunlight

roofscape has visual interest

fabric louvres absorb sound

"Double sided Pavilion"

OUTDOOR CRICKET

uniform diffuse light

INDOOR CRICKET

sides can be opened up on warm
days and for special events

light combined to form a 78 degree cut-off angle which gave the exact geometry to ensure that at 9.30 in the morning there was no possibility of direct sunlight entering the building. This configuration was simulated and tested under the artificial sky at the Bartlett School of Architecture in London with a 1:20 scale model. This proved to be an invaluable tool for both verifying assumptions made in the desk-top studies, but also as a means of allowing the sceptical cricket management to form a subjective judgement about the quality of light. A halogen lamp was used to simulate the sun and demonstrate that direct sunlight would not adversely affect the uniformity of lighting.

The brief for the Indoor Cricket School required eight nets with additional circulation space on either side. This generated a cross-section of ten bays across the width of the building which was lit by five barrel vaulted rooflights.

So, for completely different reasons, it has been found that the primary elevations of the Maplethorpe Building, the Water Polo Arena, Velvet Mill and the Indoor Cricket School at Lord's all have combinations of ten and five structural bays.

The site for the Lord's Indoor Cricket School was particularly suited to a building with a northeast-facing facade and easily accommodated a harmonious relationship between the building orientation, the movement of the sun and the time of occupation of the building. Similarly, the site at St Hugh's College allowed the Maplethorpe Building to be planned with long east- and west-facing elevations to allow all of the student rooms to have a sunny aspect for at least half of the day. However, for other building types, east- and west-facing elevations are far from desirable. For buildings such as offices and academic facilities, the most onerous environmental control challenge is to prevent overheating. If the buildings

LEFT
Analysis of the site for the Indoor School.

RIGHT
Initial concept sketch.

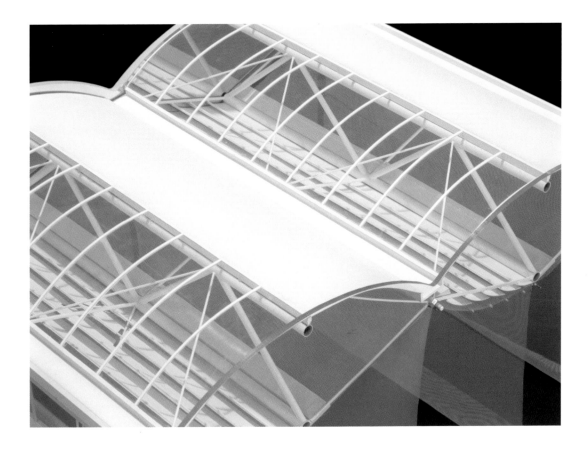

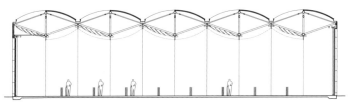

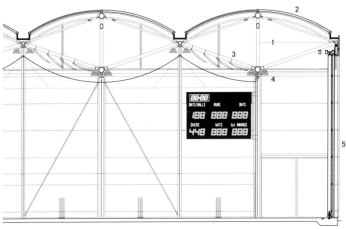

are to be predominantly naturally lit and naturally ventilated, it is critical to prevent solar gain through the building fabric. For south-facing facades this is fairly easy to achieve with horizontal projecting blinds or awnings because the sun is high in the sky. North-facing facades are generally free from direct solar radiation during the working day. However, east- and west-facing facades are subject to direct sunlight at quite low angles at critical times of day. A horizontal blind would need to be almost completely closed to keep out solar radiation and both views and daylight would be compromised. Where there is a choice, it is therefore preferable to plan the orientation of buildings to avoid this condition but, for many inner city projects, the site orientation is fixed by street patterns.

OPPOSITE
Front elevation of the Lord's Indoor Cricket School showing ratios of 5 and 3.

LEFT
1:20 scale model used to test the day lighting principles.

TOP RIGHT
Cross-section showing ratios of 8 and 5.

BOTTOM RIGHT
Detail of typical roof light module.
1 2.4 metre deep tubular steel truss.
2 Specially extruded aluminium sections supporting on one side two layers of Lexan Excell with a 70 millimetre air gap and, on the other, two layers of aluminium sheet with an insulation core.
3 Fabric blinds made from "Firesist" canvas suspended from a stainless steel cable which runs the length of the building and formed to a curve with a batten and strop.
4 Artificial up and down lights and net support trackway.
5 8 metre x 5.4 metre sliding wall panels.

View from James Street.

This presented a challenge for David Morley Architects' design for the **Rolle Building** at the University of Plymouth. The building orientation was pre-determined by the existing master plan whereby the building would define one side of a new urban space, James Square, at the heart of the University. In addition to providing general teaching spaces, the Rolle Building provides accommodation for the Faculty of Education together with other specific needs including Educational Development and Learning Technologies and Continuous Professional Development. In placing the Faculty of Education at the heart of the Plymouth campus it was intended for the new building to "break down silos" and be at the centre of a diverse and vibrant student learning experience, so the focus of learning could break out of the specialised teaching space and into a rich vocabulary of collaborative and social spaces.

The internal planning of the building required extensive consultation with user groups from the diverse mix of university departments due to occupy it. Meeting the specific needs of these departments whilst encouraging interaction between them would be critical to the success of the building. In order to accommodate the flexible range of spaces required by the brief, the Rolle Building is planned on a 1.5 metre x 1.5 metre module with a six metre x 7.5 metre structural column grid. The east side of the building takes the form of a rectangular block seven storeys high x 15 metres wide and 48 metres long. The building width was determined by the maximum dimension that would be compatible with the environmental design strategy to allow the use of natural light and ventilation. To the west, the building footprint extends out at the lower four levels to include an additional block that is aligned along James Street. The triangular

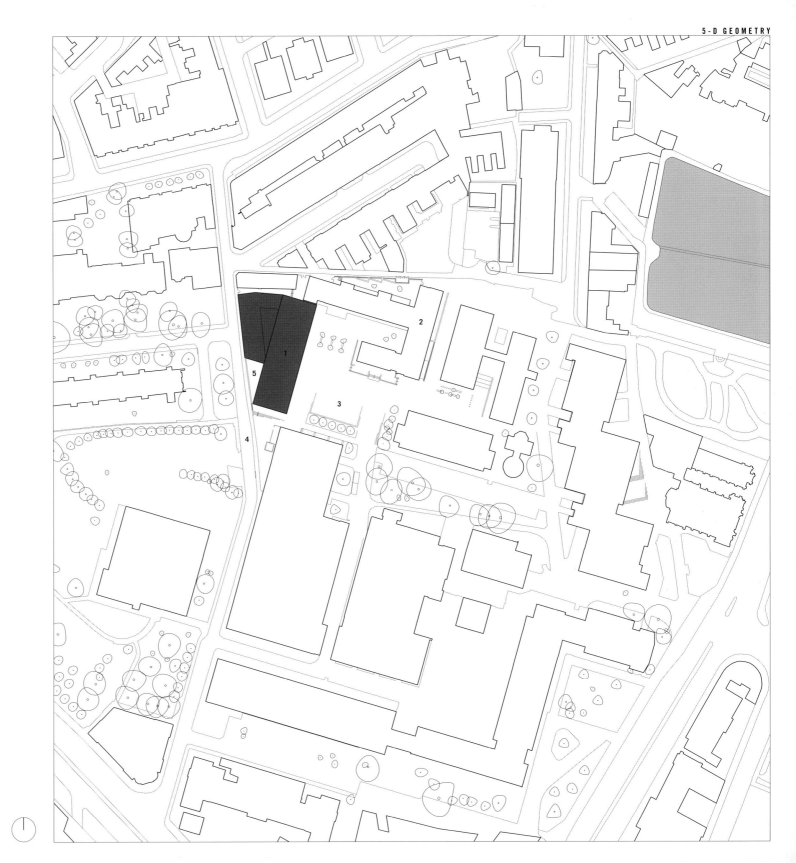

Rolle Building site plan.
1 Rolle Building
2 Student Residences
3 James Square
4 James Street
5 Pedestrian link

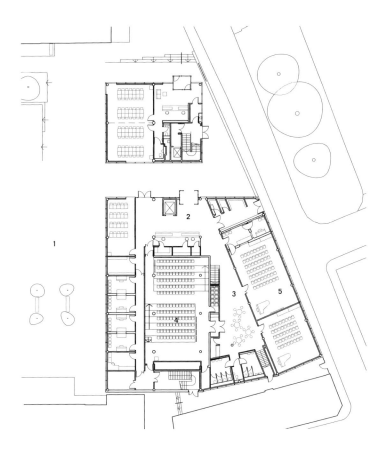

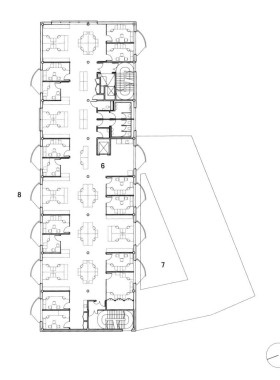

space between these two blocks form an atrium, which acts as a space for cross-fertilisation between faculties and allows light and ventilation into the deeper plan areas. At ground level there is an east to west external route that cuts through the building to reinforce links through the main spine of university activity.

The external shading to glazed areas combines aluminium *brise soleil* and horizontal louvres with bespoke curved solar shades. The geometry of the curved shade is derived from the sun path during the prime hours of occupation, giving just sufficient shade to keep direct sunlight off the windows whilst allowing views out and admitting as much daylight as possible from the diffuse part of the sky.

The geometry of this building was derived from five quite different constraints. First was the size and shape of the site. Second was the 1.5 metre planning grid driven by flexible internal planning. Third was the 7.5 metre by six metre structural grid which provides an economic reinforced concrete structure. Fourth was the town planning context, which defined the parameters for overall building height. Fifth was the network of streets and pedestrian flows which determined a cut through the building at the lower floor levels.

Although the geometry of the Rolle Building was generated in response to these independent constraints, it can be seen that there is an underlining pattern of five recurring elements. There are five planning modules in

OPPOSITE
Learning Atrium.

ABOVE
Floor plans:
Ground Floor
1 James Square
2 Entrance
3 Learning Atrium
4 Lecture hall
5 Generic teaching rooms

Sixth Floor Plan
6 Academic offices
7 Rooflight above Learning Atrium
8 Solar shades

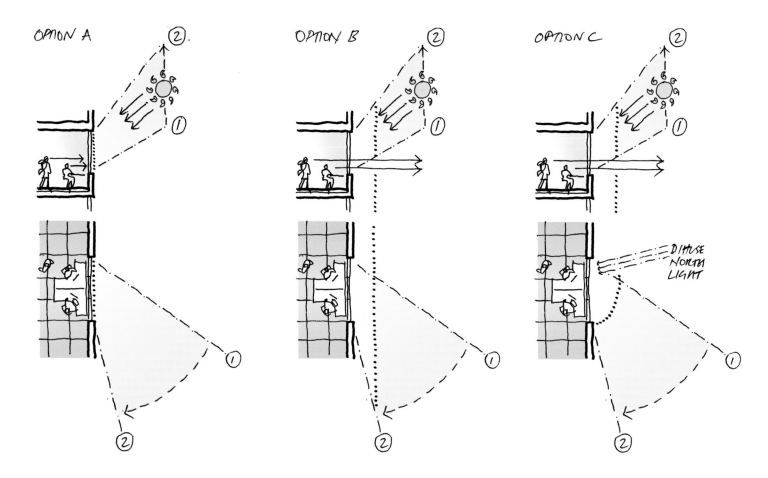

ABOVE

Design evolution of solar sails.
Option A
− Restricts view
− Restricts windows
Option B
+ Clear view
− Whole facade need shade
− More material
Option C
+ Clear view
+ Minimum material
+ Reflected light
+ Distinctive appearance

OPPOSITE

View from James Square showing the
pedestrian cut through and the solar shades.

each structural bay, there are five structural bays along the length of the building and there are five repeated storeys between the plinth of the building and the attic storey. An analysis of the principle facade also shows that the pedestrian cut through divides the facade into ratios of eight to five and five to three.

This sequence of ratios forms part of a sequence first noticed by Leonardo of Pisa, known as Fibonacci (1170–1250), where each number in the series is the sum of the preceding two numbers: 1, 2, 3, 5, 8, 13, 21 and so on. Fibonacci numbers can be observed in nature, for example in the growth patterns of leaves on a tree and the spiral forms in the head of a sunflower, a pinecone or snail. The mathematician, Alan Turing (1912–1954), who helped break the Enigma Code during the Second World War, was reputedly fascinated with the occurrence of Fibonacci

spirals in nature, known as Fibonacci phyllotaxis, "because if you can see mathematical structures in the world, it can offer a clue to the processes that generate that world".

The component parts of the Rolle Building elevation can be seen as part of a Fibonacci Spiral generated from the base module, comprising one storey height and one structural bay. The base unit of one is linked through combinations of two, three, five and eight modules to form a spiral which links together all the parts of the elevation to the whole composition.

A Fibonacci Spiral is similar to, but not identical to the Golden Spiral, which is made up of a series of nesting golden rectangles, where the ratio of one side to the next is the golden ratio. Plato defined the golden ratio as where you divide a line such that the ratio of the whole to the longer

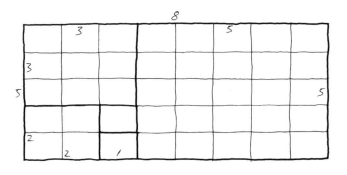

TOP LEFT
West elevation.

TOP RIGHT
Fibonacci number modules.

BOTTOM
West elevation showing Fibonacci
number modules.

equals the ratio of the longer to the shorter. This is expressed as phi where $\emptyset$ = 1.61803…. Phi is a fascinating number because $1 / \emptyset$ = 0.61803… and $\emptyset / 2$ = 2.61803….

As a Fibonacci series is extended, the ratio between one number and the next gets closer and closer to the golden ratio. For example $3 / 2$ = 1.5; $5 / 3$ = 1.667; $8 / 5$ = 1.6; $13 / 8$ = 1.625 and $21 / 13$ = 1.615. There are many references to the golden ratio occurring in nature from Leonardo Da Vinci's (1452–1519) sketches suggesting how the golden ratio recurs in the human form, to Johannes Kepler's (1571–1630) observations about the recurrence of Fibonacci numbers in leaf arrangements. Theories about the golden ratio in nature extend from the micro to the macro. Researchers have proposed connections between the golden ratio and the structure of the human genome whereby a DNA strand is exactly 34 by 21 angstroms. In 2003, Harald Weiss and Volkmar Weiss published a research paper that concluded from an analysis of psychometric data that the golden ratio underlies the clock cycle of brain waves. On the macro scale, Scott Olsen tells us in his book on the golden section that "Nature's greatest secret that rotating black holes flip from a negative to a positive heat when the specific heat of the square of the mass to the square of the spin parameter[3] is in the golden ratio."

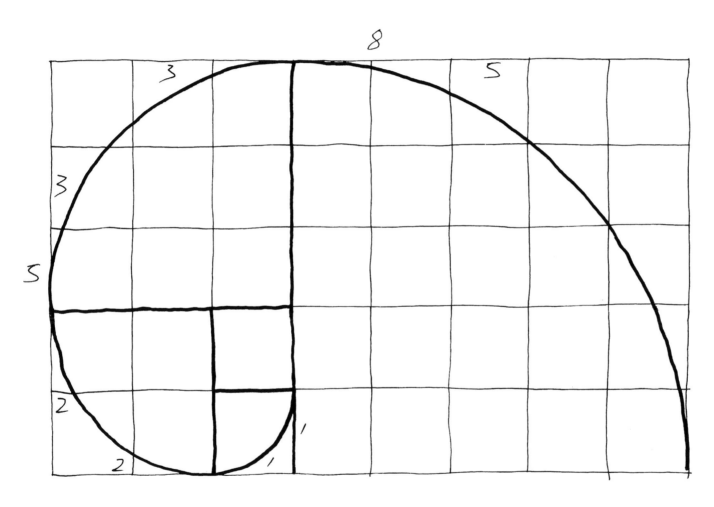

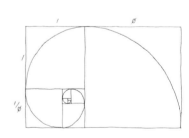

Adolf Zeising (1810–1876) introduced the concept that "the Golden Section was the proportion pervading Macrocosm and Microcosm alike",[4] and this was picked up by the architect, Hendrick Berlage (1856–1934), who applied a system of proportion at the Amsterdam Exchange which consisted of a three-dimensional network of "Egyptian Triangles which generated golden rectangles on the facade".[5] There is evidence to suggest that Charles-Édouard Jeanneret, better known as Le Corbusier (1887–1965) was familiar with the work of Zeising and Berlage and both the Golden ratio and the Fibonacci numbers form a central part to his proportional system set out in "the Modulor", 1954.[6]

The Modulor comprised two series of dimensions based on the Fibonacci series called the "Red Series" and the "Blue Series". Both were derived from the proportions of the human body epitomised by the Modulor man. Le Corbusier wanted the system to translate easily from centimetres to inches, because he saw the centimetre as an inhuman measurement. The dimensions were generated from the height of the Modulor man, taken as six foot or 182.88 centimetre, equivalent to the height of the English policeman.[7] The Red Series is the same as the Blue Series multiplied by a factor of two. Le Corbusier proclaimed that the natural qualities of his measurements were proven by the fact that they could be converted into whole numbers of half inches, a measurement system derived from the

LEFT
Fibonacci Spiral.

RIGHT
Golden Spiral.

LEFT
Leonardo da Vinci proposed that the golden ratio occurs in key proportions of the human form.

RIGHT
Fibonacci numbers revealed in Morley's analysis of a pine cone showing eight clockwise spirals and 13 anti-clockwise spirals.

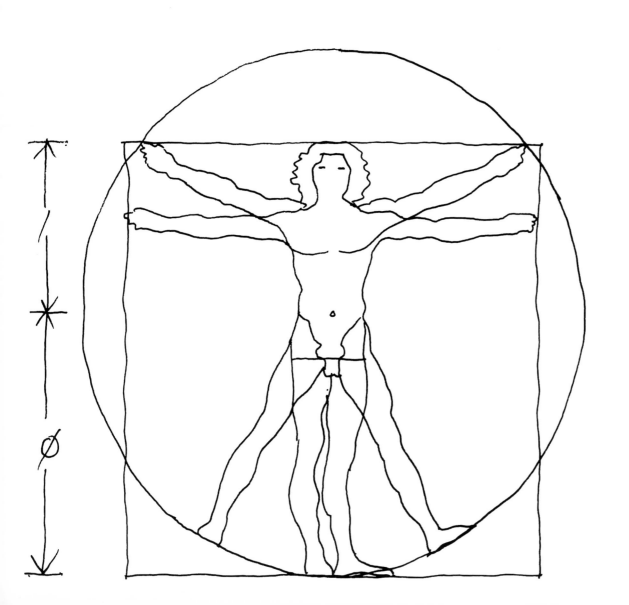

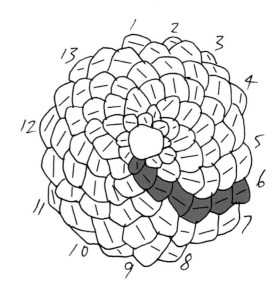

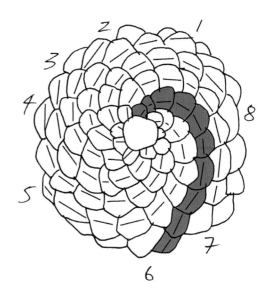

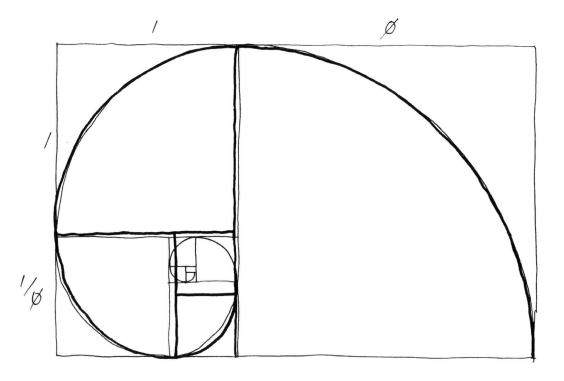

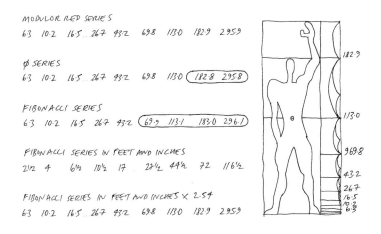

MODULOR RED SERIES
6·3   10·2   16·5   26·7   43·2   69·8   113·0   182·9   295·9

∅ SERIES
6·3   10·2   16·5   26·7   43·2   69·8   113·0   (182·8   295·8)

FIBONACCI SERIES
6·3   10·2   16·5   26·7   43·2   (69·9   113·1   183·0   296·1)

FIBONACCI SERIES IN FEET AND INCHES
2½   4   6½   10½   17   27½   44½   72   116½

FIBONACCI SERIES IN FEET AND INCHES × 2·54
6·3   10·2   16·5   26·7   43·2   69·8   113·0   182·9   295·9

human body. On closer analysis the claimed similarity, far from being a coincidence, was actually a consequence of the Modulor being generated from the outset in feet and inches and then converted to centimetres, as proved by Morley in 1977.[8]

This anecdote illustrates a tension between a proportional system based on irrational numbers and the need, in most forms of construction, for repetitive modules. In this respect the Fibonacci numbers, since they are whole rational numbers, are of particular interest.

An overlay of the Fibonacci Spiral onto the Golden Spiral reveals that within the range three, five, and eight the Fibonacci Spiral approximates very closely to the Golden Spiral whereas the spiral generated by the lower Fibonacci numbers, one, two and three noticeably diverges. It is also notable that, the spiral generated by the higher Fibonacci numbers 13, 21 and so on does not increase the correlation of the two spirals by a significant amount. Furthermore, the higher Fibonacci numbers are limited in their application in buildings since they have more limited

potential for sub-divisibility. This shows that, as a basis for a system of proportion, the ratios found in the series three, five and eight are sufficient to generate almost exact golden ratios (between 97 and 99 per cent accuracy). The ratio of three to five is 1.666… and five to eight is 1.6. Of particular interest is that the central figure in this mini-series of three, five and eight is the number five. Could this be why five repeated modules are so frequently observed in David Morley Architects' projects?

In 1977 David Morley devised a proportional system called "Practically Modulor" which was practically the same as the Modulor but was more practical, being comprised of dimensions of components commonly available in the supply chain, and utilising just the lower end of the Fibonacci series to generate proportional relationships. Higher numbers of modules were generated by simply doubling or trebling the Fibonacci range three, five and eight to give six, ten and 16 or nine, 15 or 24. This is a similar principle to a musical composition where a rhythm of notes are established within an octave band and, for a higher and lower pitch, the same notes are used but in a higher or lower octave.

LEFT
Proof that the only way of deriving the exact Modulor numbers is by deriving the series in inches and then converting the series to centimetres.

RIGHT
Comparison of Fibonacci Spiral and Golden Spiral.

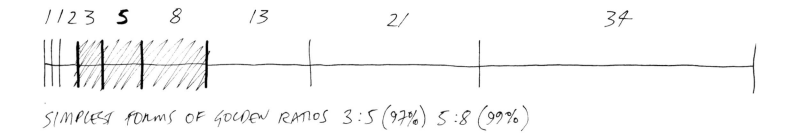

SIMPLEST FORMS OF GOLDEN RATIOS 3:5 (97%) 5:8 (99%)

ABOVE
The most useful range of Fibonacci numbers generating both a golden ratio and being useful construction modules.

OPPOSITE
5 is at the centre of a simple geometric construction of the golden ratio.

The pivotal nature of the number five in a system of harmonious proportions is reinforced by considering the mathematical equation that describes the golden ratio which is $Ø = (\sqrt{5} + 1)$ or alternatively $1 / Ø = (\sqrt{5} - 1)$. Furthermore a simple geometric construction of the golden ratio is arrived at by placing five points at equal spaces around the circumference of a circle. The ratio between the lengths of any line connecting any point will be either one to one or one to phi, the golden ratio.

Does this matter for architecture? Interest in the golden section, dating back to Plato, has certainly gone in and out of fashion. The architect Sir John Soane (1753–1837) expressed the view that "Taste, good sense and sound judgment must direct the mind of the architect to apply harmony and justice of relative proportion"[9] and Christopher Alexander wrote about the analysis of proportions in a building "both the lines of the analyses and the beadings, mouldings, frames, etc., of the object itself are so thick, (in relation to the object's overall dimensions) and the intersections can be so variously made, that any subsequent deductions and results are valueless".[10] However, as recently as 2012, Manchester University and the Manchester Science Festival are seeking to revive Alan Turing's investigation into one of the great mysteries of nature: how complex shapes and patterns arise from simple balls of cells. In a world of information overload, the concept of finding simple patterns underlying complex forms has a considerable attraction.

Five has been shown to be a central Fibonacci number and also the number from which golden ratios can be derived. In "Natural Consequences", the definition of five natural elements was observed in several different cultures and, in nature itself, five can be observed not just as part of Fibonacci Spirals but also in many flowers such as the rose or violet.[11] Cut open an apple and observe the five pips. In music a score is composed using five staves and the perfect fifth is considered more consonant, or stable, than any other interval except the unison and the octave. Counting systems developed independently by cultures such as the Romans and Mayans used sequences of five. In "Tuning In" five is deployed in several ways in the process of communication.

Having observed the frequent occurrence of the number five in nature, having noted its importance in harmonious ratios established by Fibonacci Series and the golden ratio and having seen it recurring in David Morley Architects' buildings, where does this lead for the next generation of buildings? Five was never considered to be a starting point in a design, it was, in a sense, the "Natural Consequence". For the future, five is proposed as a reference point, in the knowledge that it can be simply linked with harmonious proportions back to unity on the one hand or projected forward to infinity on the other. 5-D Geometry therefore suggests considering the geometry of shape and form in how it relates to nature and by so doing, connecting man with the environment in the broadest sense. It suggests a further dimension to geometry which is about combining practical construction with the spirit of a place.[12]

1. This sequence of numbers, where each number in the series is the sum of the preceding two numbers, was first noticed by Fibonacci (1170–1250).

2. The C value is defined in the "Guide to safety at Sports Grounds", published by the Department for Culture Media and Sport, as the assumed height, in millimetres between the top of the head and the theoretical eye height of a spectator. The higher the value, the better the sightline. C60 is not uncommon in football stadia and C90 is the standard set for the Olympic Games. C200 is recommended at Royal Ascot where spectators are prone to wear hats.

3. The spin parameter of a black hole is a unitless quantity between nought and one, nought being a static black hole and one being the most extreme black hole.

4. This interpretation was taken from Professor Wittkower, "Le Corbusier's Modulor", in *Le Corbusier in Perspective*, Harlow: Prentice Hall, 1975, p. 87.

5. Berlage's Egyptian triangles were pointed out by Pieter Singelenburg in *H P Berlage*, 1972, p.113 . He also noted that the "Egyptian Triangle was given coverage by Viollet-le-Duc, who referred to them as '*generateurs des proportions*'".

6. See "Le Corbusier's Theory of Proportion", by Morley, 1977, held in the Cambridge University Department of Architecture.

7. Le Corbusier stated "Have you ever noticed that in English detective novels, the good-looking men, such as the policemen, are always six feet tall?", *Modulor*, p. 56.

8. "Le Corbusier's Theory of Proportion", Morley, 1977.

9. Soane, John, *Lectures on Architecture*, 1929, p 100.

10. Alexander, Christopher, "Perception and Modular Coordination", in, *RIBA Journal*, October 1959.

11. See Keith Critchlow's *The Hidden Geometry of Flowers*, 2011.

12. Le Corbusier, in his *Last Works* reflecting on the application of the Modulor wrote "I have been inspired by one single pre-occupation… to introduce into the home the sense of the sacred", p. 174.

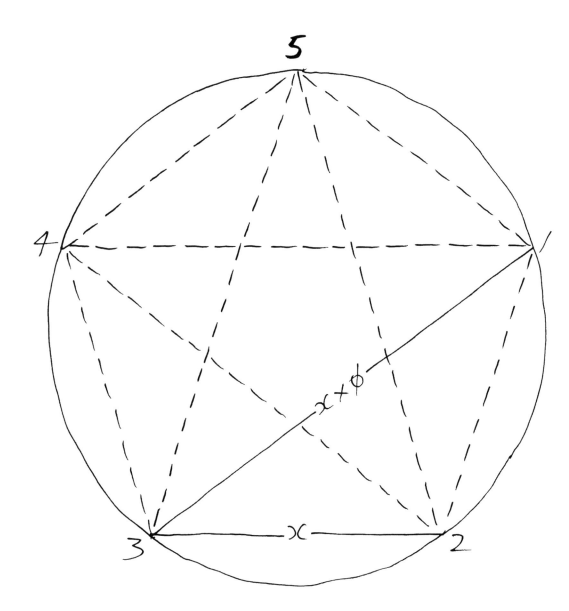

SIMPLE DERIVATION OF Ø FROM 'FIVE'

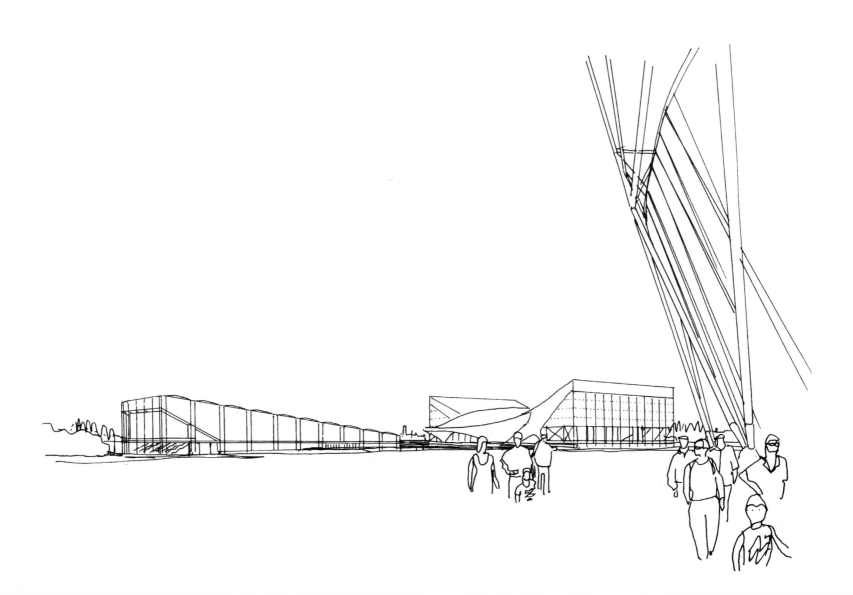

I'm writing this on the day that the Shard in London is officially opened, and as usual the public debate has focused on the obvious questions: how tall is it, how much did it cost, who designed it and do people like it or not. But less scrutinised are the reasons for it: who paid for it, who built it, and why. The process at the heart of change in the city is as much to do with whether a myriad of individual clients make good or bad decisions and so, a better or worse place.

At the Olympic Delivery Authority I had the privilege of working with a number of exceptional British architects, including David Morley Architects, who have provided London with some outstanding buildings that will reinforce the often heard view that Britain is uniquely blessed with extraordinary design talent. But it was no accident that the ODA created an Olympic Park of such quality; the organisation set out with the intent to be a good client, knowing the value of good design and recognising the benefits of achieving it.

Apart from the obvious point that to get a good design you must appoint a good architect; but there is more to it, good design is both a product and a process simultaneously and one cannot be divorced from the other. In the process, it is the client that has to lead and focus on getting the best from the team. In particular spending enough time at the right time. At the ODA an early decision was made to split the programme into three parts, Planning, Building, Testing. Two years were allocated to 'Planning' including the design stage. The pressure was on from the outset to break ground early and push forward design quickly but the ODA resisted the temptation to speed up the design stages, recognising that time spent early would be well spent, getting the procurement of teams right, getting the priorities established, and then allowing the appointed teams to develop their designs, to assess all the options and to unravel the briefs and determine the clarifying factors—a process that allowed the emergence of the sightlines in Water Polo as one of the governing principles that underpins the design. It was this focus on allowing the time early in the project that gave increasing certainty overall on the programme and budget. The more that can be explored and resolved on paper, the more certainty there is that the construction will run smoothly, that the building will do what it is required to do by its users and that the investment has therefore been made wisely.

It is at the beginning of the design process where the value is really added. A good client will create an environment in which the time can be taken to explore many possibilities, establishing what works best. Not being too certain too soon, allowing discussion to take its course and being open to dialogue. Communication takes listening skills on both sides; there's architecture which is iconic and pre-determined and there's architecture which is useful and reflective. The skill of the architect is in listening and then creating opportunities to discuss further and honing into a solution that is informed by increasing conviction.

SELINA MASON

PREVIOUS PAGES
As part of the process of tuning in all staff at David Morley Architects meet every Monday to discuss the week ahead.

OPPOSITE
Initial sketch for the London 2012 Water Polo Arena (left) shown in the context of the Olympic Stadium (right) and the Aquatics Centre (middle).

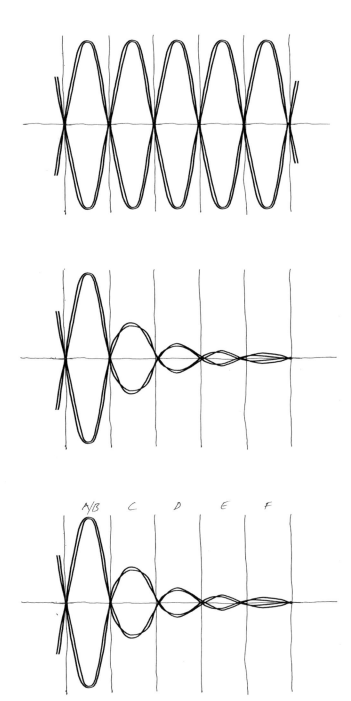

TOP
Analogy of radio waves with the iterative process of design.

MIDDLE
Diagram of the iterative process tuning in to a focussed solution.

BOTTOM
Organisation of "Tuning In" process into work stages as prescribed by the RIBA:
A/B Inception and feasibility
C   Sketch design
D   Detailed design
E   Technical design
F   Production information

The last chapter concluded that 5-D Geometry was a tool to help architecture to connect people to their environment. This chapter is about the process of communication necessary to ensure that the outcome of a design is clearly focused on the needs of society. In the "Foreword" the derivation of Five by 5 was covered: "Using the terminology from Voice Communication protocols adopted for radio transmission, where the signal quality is reported on two scales; the first for signal strength, the second for signal clarity; these scales range from one to five, where one is the worst and five is the best. The listening station reports these numbers separated with the word 'by'. 'Five by five' therefore means a signal that has excellent strength and perfect clarity—the most understandable signal possible." Continuing the analogy with radio transmission, design can be thought of as a process of tuning in to find the optimum signal. A project begins with some form of loosely defined need and the design process follows a series of iterations to more closely define the brief and the best possible design response. In the same way as twiddling the knob of a radio to find the right station, the design process follows a series of gradually more focused iterations, exploring the range of possibilities and homing in on the preferred solution.

Like tuning a radio, in order to successfully find a well focussed design solution, a sufficient range of possibilities need to be explored and feedback needs to be carefully listened to. It is therefore important to think laterally at the outset of a project and consult widely to get as much feedback as possible. Following the theme of Five by 5 communications the tuning in process can be plotted on a diagram where the strength of the design solution is measured on the x axis and the clarity along the y axis. In this way the design process begins by oscillating between the unknown and absolute clarity. However, after each iteration, something has been learnt and the design gets progressively stronger. The bandwidths of the oscillations can reduce as the design solution becomes increasingly clear.

There is a parallel here with the progression illustrated in the previous chapter whereby the ratios of a Fibonacci Series progressively tend towards the golden ratio. It is notable that within five steps the Fibonacci sequence has approximated towards the golden ratio within an accuracy of 0.4 per cent. David Morley Architects structure the design process in a similar way. There are five main steps of the design process, as set out in the Royal Institute of British Architects (RIBA) Standard Form of Appointment for an Architect or similar systems adopted worldwide.

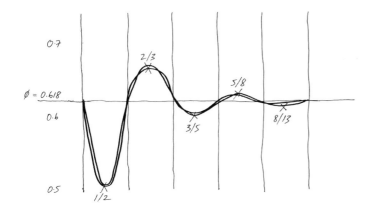

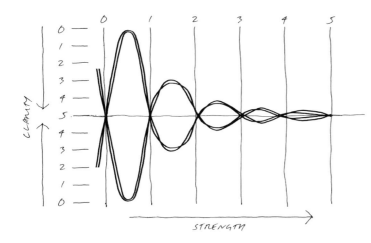

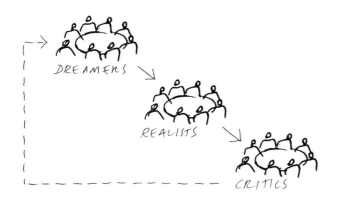

These comprise the Feasibility Study comprising an initial appraisal and preparation of the design brief (Stages A and B), the Concept (Stage C), the Design Development (Stage D), the Technical Design (Stage E) and the Production Information (Stage F). Like the Fibonacci Series, after five stages the iterative process has become sufficiently focussed. In order to control this process, the iterative process is brought to a close at the end of each work stage and an integrated set of information is produced for comment by all stakeholders before the next stage begins.

So how does the iterative process work? It is generally recognised that the complexity of many problems facing architects today is beyond the limits of an individual's logic and intuition to solve. Complexity is compounded where an initial brief is often ill-defined and where increasingly rapid developments of materials technologies and legislation need to be taken into account. In Christopher Alexander's *Notes on the Synthesis of Form* he suggests a way of breaking down complex design problems into a hierarchy of sub-problems, which become simple enough to be addressed logically. On the other hand Bruce Archer (1922–2005), Professor of Design Research at the Royal College of Art, in *Whatever became of Design Methodology*, recognised that "It is widely accepted, I think, that design problems are characterised by being ill-defined. An ill-defined problem is one in which the requirements, as given, do not contain sufficient information to enable the designer to arrive at a means of meeting those requirements simply by transforming, reducing, optimising or superimposing the given information alone." He goes on to suggest a design process based on experimentation and selection through empirical research. David Morley Architects' tuning in process combines both Alexander's and Archers' approaches and recognises that the efficiency of design is driven by using the right method at the right point in the process.

There is, however, another process to consider in addition to periods of logical analysis interspersed with periods of optioneering and evaluation and that is generating sparks of creativity and lateral thinking. Creative ideas often come unpredictably and that complicates the business of architecture, which is usually bounded by strict timescales and deadlines. It is therefore important to create the right settings for creativity to happen. Following the radio analogy, this means removing the background noise. Walt Disney recognised this and is said to have structured his creative activities through a series of teams in different rooms where the first team are dreamers who think in an everything is possible mode,

TOP
Representation of the Fibonacci Series progressing towards the golden ratio.

MIDDLE
The "Tuning In" process using the terminology of "Five by 5".

BOTTOM
Disney's three rooms.

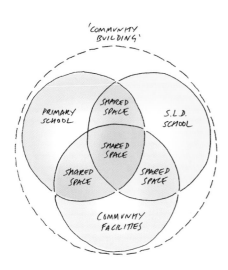

"A SCHOOL IS A COMMUNITY BUILDING WHICH HAPPENS TO BE USED FOR EDUCATION"

LEFT
Concept for The Campus.

RIGHT
Site strategy sketch showing a five bay, two-storey high, deep plan flexible enclosure bounded by curved structures that bring down the scale at either end to relate to the surrounding residential context.

the second team are realists who know all of the constraints and select options which are most likely to succeed and the third are critics who look for problems and then, if necessary, send the ideas back to the dreamers to begin a process of refinement. The broad bandwidth of the tuning in process therefore needs to accommodate all of these modes of thinking.

The analogy of the design process to tuning in pre-supposes there is a signal to tune in to or, in other words, that each project has a best possible outcome waiting to be found. It could be argued that a project brief may have no solution, but this is dealt with by the wording "best possible outcome". Through an iterative process, a project brief will need to evolve in response to feedback about what is, and what is not, feasible, thus ensuring that a best possible outcome can indeed be found. This reinforces the need for breadth in initial thinking so that opportunities are not ruled out through a lack of imagination.

It might also be suggested that a project brief has more than one "best possible outcome". This again makes the breadth of early consultation critical, by establishing a picture of what is "best" in the minds of all the stakeholders involved with the project and, beyond that, what

is best for society as a whole. This requires a carefully managed process of communication and dialogue aimed at establishing at the beginning of a project the criteria by which it will be judged as a success on completion. Steadman, in *The Evolution of Designs* points out that "what are often regarded as 'unavoidable' requirements of function, or limitations of material, are in fact matters of intentional choice on the part of the maker". He has recognised that, in reality, the definition of a problem to be solved is not fixed at the outset and evolves through an iterative process taking on board feedback from the developing design. The following examples show how that process has worked on five David Morley Architects projects.

The inspiration for **The Campus** project in Locking Castle, Weston-Super-Mare, came from a vision about how schools fit into society. The brief was to provide primary education facilities for what was reckoned to be the largest housing development in Europe. The client was North Somerset Council and this was their first school built since their inception in 1997, so they had high ambitions for it to exemplify a vision for future schools. The brief included a new primary school for 420 children, a 26 place nursery; an integrated 67 place severe learning disabilities school catering for three to 19 year olds; an adult education college and a host

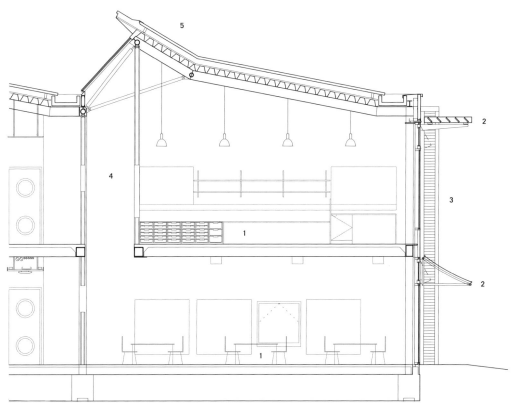

of community facilities from a library to a skate park to be provided on a constrained site adjacent to the commercial centre of Locking Castle.

The commission came through an architectural competition but with the opportunity for one-to-one dialogue as part of the competition process. There is often a dilemma when participating in architectural competitions because there is limited scope to engage in the iterative process necessary to properly tune in. Often the inspiration for a project comes, not from a written brief, but from conversation and dialogue. In this case it was with Russ Currie, North Somerset Council's project leader, who said that in his view "a school should be a community building that just happens to be used for education". This elegant inversion of the normal way that schools are conceived stimulated the dream for the Campus, one building with five different functions, which would maximise the overlaps so that the building could be used intensively for 365 days a year.

This vision was explored through a series of diagrams to show how a mix of community facilities could be interconnected to maximise sharing whilst also allowing the five key users: mainstream school children; severe learning disabilities school; community uses; adult education and conferences to operate securely and independently. To achieve

successful room adjacencies a building diagram was developed with shared facilities such as a dining hall and sports hall in the centre surrounded by the schools and community facilities in a way that allows each to expand and contract into the shared areas according to the time of day or week. With a very limited site these adjacencies could only be achieved with a very deep plan. This was at odds with the demands of a naturally lit and naturally ventilated school, which would normally have a shallow plan. Still at competition stage, the tuning in process was extended to bring in Neil Smith from environmental engineers Max Fordham LLP and Andy Toohey from structural engineers Price and Myers, to explore if a very deep plan building could be made to work as a low energy building. A solution was found where a two-storey high steel framed envelope with beam and block mezzanine floors could be engineered with a roof which would allow north light and fresh air to penetrate the variety of spaces below. Reflective light shafts bring daylight down to the lower level of double-stacked classrooms and allow natural cross-ventilation to be achieved, using the stack effect of the light shafts. The deep plan arrangement allowed a compact footprint for the building to be developed which had considerable advantages for the site planning, whereby the building could be used to define a new town square and a focal point for the community.

LEFT
View of the entrance plaza of the completed building showing the curving roof of the community centre with the flexible shared school spaces beyond and the smaller structure for the nursery in the distance.

RIGHT
Cross-section through classroom wing.
1 Classroom
2 Projecting sun shades
3 Ventilation shafts with acoustic attenuation
4 Reflective light and ventilation shafts
5 Space for photovoltaic panels

LEFT
View of the completed naturally-lit shared schools foyer space.

RIGHT
South-facing classroom facade showing projecting sun shades and acoustically attenuated natural ventilation louvres.

OPPOSITE TOP
Initial sketch for the shared schools foyer space.

OPPOSITE BOTTOM
Detail of acoustically attenuated natural ventilation louvres.

1 Fresh air enters between aluminium louvres lined with acoustic quilt
2 2.1 metre high insulated aluminium panel opens for acoustically attenuated natural ventilation
3 203 millimetre Steel Universal Column with intumescent paint finish
4 Rainwater downpipe
5 Western Red Cedar timber cladding with shiplap profile

A toplit open plan dining room lies at the heart of the building and can be shared by both the schools and community. This flexible space has moveable walls so that it can be used as a foyer to the gymnasium for events or separately hired for social gatherings in addition to the everyday uses of dining and assembly. All classroom windows face south, with projecting canopies and louvres that help control summer sun and allow some free heat from the low winter sun. The roof pitch varies to accommodate northlights and panels for future photovoltaic tiles that will cater for the energy needs of the classrooms. A particular issue was reconciling the demanding requirements regarding noise control and ventilation with a low-energy approach.

Because the building fronts directly onto the road, it was necessary to keep road noise down to comply with the stricter building regulations concerning background noise in classrooms. This normally leads to a mechanically ventilated solution but here, by combining the intuition of the mechanical engineer and the expertise of an acoustician, an alternative low energy solution was found. It comprises a series of full-height doors in the corner of each classroom which can be opened up to admit fresh air through two rows of vertical louvres lined with acoustically absorbent materials for noise attenuation. This allows the classrooms to be insulated from any perceptible outdoor noise, even when the ventilation panels are fully open.

The competition proposals were presented as a series of freehand sketches, an essential tool in the tuning in process to communicate ideas without committing to detail. The relationship to the urban context and the flexibility of the plan form won the unanimous support of the competition assessors, who included the local authority, the town council and representatives from the new schools. Following on from that, the iterative process of developing the brief and testing design solutions extended to smaller interactive workshops with staff, parents and children and continued throughout the design and construction. The children loved being engaged in the process and struck up a rapport with the contractor who they referred to as "Bob the Builder", and who in return made them a "sheep pen" on the site so they could watch the building take shape. As with many school projects the process of consultation extended well beyond the client to include a broad range of representatives of the community. An exhibition was set up in the

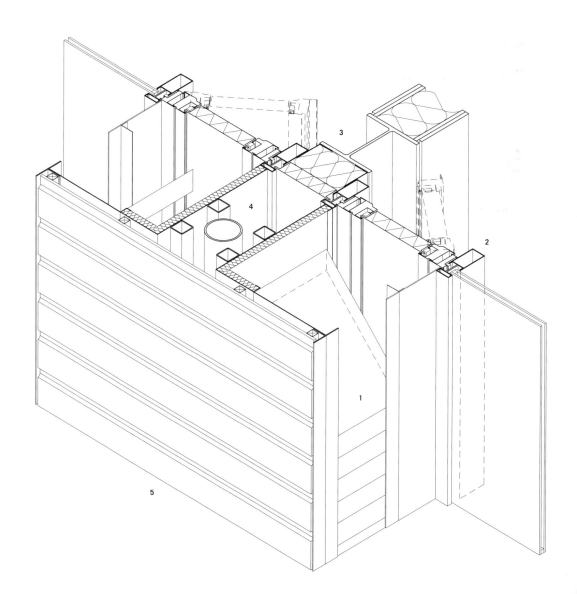

LEFT
At one end of the building the scale breaks down to give a smaller scale space for the Special Learning Needs Nursery.

OPPOSITE
At the other end of the building the Community facilities open onto a new town square.

local supermarket and for this, fly-through animations were found to be a particularly successful communication tool. One of the points emerging from the consultation was the potential benefit of the supermarket being so close to the school whereby drop-off and collection could be synchronised with shopping for essential supplies.

The Campus has two main entrances, one for the community facilities and one for school use. Barrie Evans wrote in *The Architects' Journal*: "In contrast to the design of many new schools, The Campus opens its doors on to the pavement, rather than being enclosed behind fencing and gates.

There is obviously a perimeter fence for security reasons, but the building itself is part of it. This creates a sense of openness to the community, a sense that it is there for all to use, rather than for a select few."[1] This sense of openness is reinforced by full-height glazing to the double-height reception, library and meeting rooms. These spaces are enclosed with a sweeping roof which brings the scale down to just a single storey where it faces the adjacent low-rise housing, avoiding any overlooking issues. The entrance to the school is less open, fronted with masonry, giving a more protected environment. A generous canopy provides a sheltered area where minibuses can drop off pupils for the severe learning difficulties school.

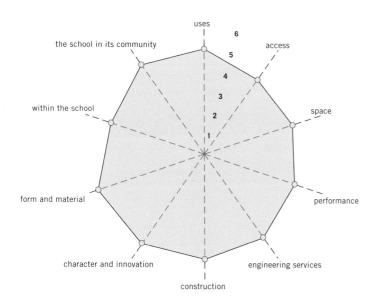

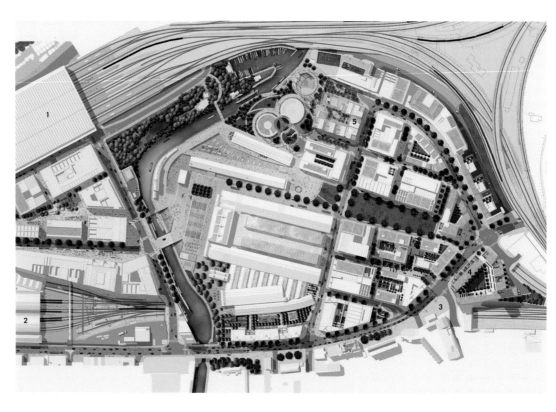

LEFT
The Campus Design Quality Indicator
Assessment 'Spider'.

RIGHT
Initial master plan for King's Cross Central
development by Allies and Morrison and
Porphyrios Associates with Townshends
Landscape Architects.
1 St Pancras Station
2 King's Cross Station
3 York Way
4 Triangle site
5 P1 site

The process of tuning in involves listening to, and incorporating, feedback at all stages of a project and this includes when the building is in use. At The Campus a post-occupancy review was measured through formal "Design Quality Indicators" which reflect the breadth of issues to be considered throughout a project. A lesson learnt from The Campus was that for future projects, the process of post-occupancy review should be initiated at the outset of the project and reviewed during the course of the design. This approach is being promoted by the Building Services Research and Information Association (BSRIA) as part of their so-called "Soft Landings" framework which is referred to later in this chapter.

David Morley Architects' work at King's Cross Central has included various projects with particular similarities to The Campus. Here the process of tuning in required a more subtle process of consultation since the context for the projects comprised a series of undeveloped sites with projects being designed by different architects in varying stages of evolution and flux. The developer, Argent, with a team of consultants including master plan architects Allies and Morrison and Porphyrios Associates have drawn up a vision to create a vibrant and mixed-use new urban quarter that is currently being developed on 67 acres of land at King's Cross, in the heart of London. In 2001 they published their vision under the banner of "Principles for a Human City" as the first part of an on-going process of consultation and dialogue that is still continuing. They have engaged, so far, 21 architectural practices to explore the potential of 47 new buildings, ten new squares and 20 new streets. Initially sketch designs were prepared for each site to help define parameters that have formed the basis for consultation and then an outline planning approval. This formed a flexible basis for the subsequent development of each site

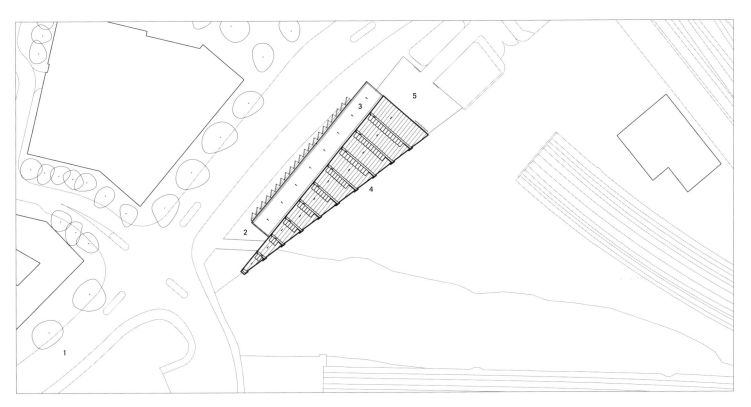

with more detailed designs as requirements evolved and opportunities came forward. The master plan makes good use of several fine industrial structures which served the former use of the land as a railway goods yard and this provides a good historical reference for the new urban fabric. However, the richness of the emerging new cityscape is also a product of the multiplicity of designers who have been involved and the manner in which Argent have allowed them to respond and react to their emerging designs in a dynamic and collaborative manner. This process of dialogue and communication has created a sense of organic development that would more typically be associated with a historic city.

In the initial stage David Morley Architects' input was to explore sketch proposals for a triangular site for residential, commercial and leisure facilities to the north of the regeneration area, known as the "Triangle Site"

The awkwardly shaped site was further complicated since it has a one-storey level difference across its length and it is bisected by the boundary between Camden and Islington Borough Councils. The Borough boundary used to follow the line of a major road, York Way, which has since been re-aligned as part of the wider regeneration project. Of all the sites at King's Cross, the Triangle Site will be one of the last to be developed and is the only site which is not fully in Camden. Argent decided that it would therefore make a good temporary home for a facility to train local people to become construction workers for the remainder of the re-development. This laudable initiative subsequently became a condition of the outline planning approval issued by Camden Council and therefore the site became even more complicated because the building had to be within the acute triangular slither that lay within the Camden boundary.[2] The **King's Cross Construction Skills Centre** therefore became one of the first schemes

TOP
The entrance bridge brings visitors into an entrance foyer at first floor level.

BOTTOM
King's Cross Construction Skills Centre site plan.
1 York Way
2 Entrance bridge
3 Classroom block
4 Workshops
5 Loading bay

Entrance detail and York Way elevation. The 15,600 square foot facility provides more than double the space required in the Section 106 agreement with the London Borough of Camden.

to be built at the King's Cross regeneration project. Like The Campus, it is a two-storey semi-industrial building with northlights supporting photo-voltaic panels, natural light and natural ventilation. The design is intended to embody the principles of quality and sustainability that underlie Argent's scheme by encouraging the mixing of both occupants and visitors. The building's purpose is to enhance construction skills and encourage people to join the industry and so an unmissable entrance was created at the highest and pointed end of the thin triangular site. The entrance is screened from the adjacent undeveloped land and made more prominent by a screen of high visibility yellow perforated metal, echoing the colour of the 'high viz' vests which are the obligatory uniform for the trainees. By entering the building at first floor level the entrance foyer becomes a viewing gallery down into the large double-height workshop, highlighting the purpose of the building from the point of entry. The classrooms are also at the entrance level and have views down into the workshop, reinforcing the relationship between theory and practice. The detailing is intended as a construction lesson for the students. Ceiling soffits are exposed, as are the services and, where possible, wall systems. The plant room is caged, and the workshop and stair floors are in exposed concrete. A timber *brise-soleil* protects the west-facing office and classroom windows from

solar gain while providing a clear view of the sky to the north. All areas except toilets are naturally ventilated. A sedum roof supports biodiversity and some passive cooling to the adjacent photovoltaic panels. Appropriately, the trainees have built their own canteen alongside the supervisors' offices. Stephanie Fischer, in *Architecture Today* noted that in her conversations with trainees from the Construction Skills Centre "They liked the consistency of materials in the building as well as being able to see how it had been built. And they took particular pride in having built elements of the fit-out as part of their training."[3]

Since this is a temporary building, like the Water Polo Venue featured in "Natural Consequences", affordability was important as was the need to construct the building quickly. The tuning in process therefore involved a very early engagement with the supply chain, exploring key strategic issues such as the benefits of a component-based scheme versus rented modular construction. In this case, the contractor was also the client and the end user, therefore simplifying the breadth of consultation required. The importance of post-occupancy feedback has already been highlighted with The Campus. The King's Cross Construction Skills Centre goes one step further, whereby the building itself is giving feedback to its users.

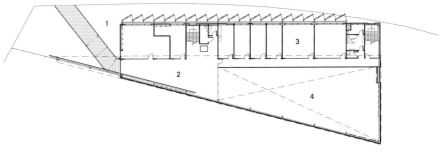

LEFT
The west-facing louvres are canted at an angle to admit unobstructed daylight from the northwest.

RIGHT
Long section and first floor plan:
1 Entrance bridge
2 Entrance foyer
3 Classroom gallery
4 Workshops
5 Northlights and photovoltaic panels.

LEFT
The double-height workshop is lit from a
sawtooth roof which provides northlight and
supports south-facing photovoltaic panels. As
the process of tuning in moves from sketch
ideas through to increasingly firm proposals,
Morley's approach is for the communication
technique to match the process—a freehand
sketch is open to interpretation and allows
the consultee to focus on the important
issues without being distracted by details.
Using the analogy of radio communication
it is aiming to communicate without the
interference of background noise.

RIGHT
View of the completed double-height
workshop.

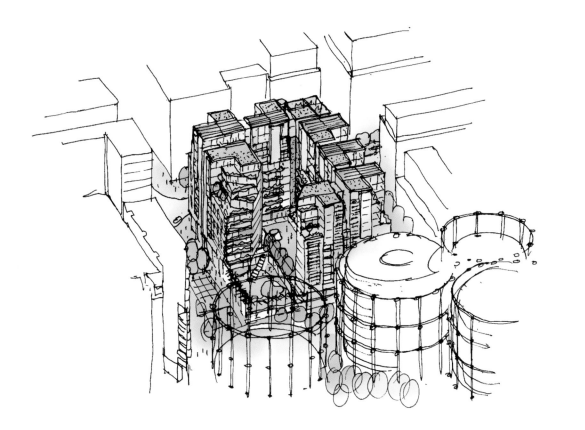

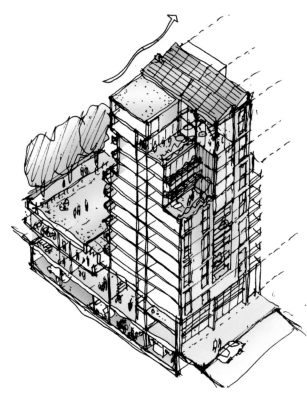

The second David Morley Architects project at King's Cross Central is known as the **P1 Building**. The proposals will provide a new living quarter comprising open market and key worker residential accommodation, located above a learning environment that will bring together a school for deaf and hard of hearing children, a new mainstream primary school and nursery and community facilities all under one roof.

The building is conceived as a cluster of domestic-scaled towers arranged around a central garden. The footprint extends to the edge of the site and clearly defines the adjacent streets. The school and community facilities occupy a two-storey plinth at the base of the building, where they will create an active frontage, with 11 storeys of residential accommodation above. The perimeter of the development is punctuated on the southwest

corner to allow long views out across the Regent's Canal and to permit as much daylight and sunlight as possible to be brought into the heart of the site. The open corner accommodates, at ground level, the playground and outdoor learning spaces for the school. This arrangement creates good adjacencies with a recreational multi-use games area beneath the neighbouring building accessible across a traffic free "Home Zone".[4] A central garden provides a focal point for the apartments above and contains rooflights which are integrated as sculptural features within the landscape design allowing daylight to flood into the circulation spaces of the deep plan school below. The garden is conceived as a three-dimensional oasis of greenery and extends to the full height of the building through a combination of trees, vertical climbing plants and informal planting on balconies. This will define a lush green theme to

LEFT
Study of a typical tower showing set-backs above the ninth floor to improve daylight in the adjacent street.

RIGHT
Initial concept sketch for the P1 Site showing a cluster of towers around a central garden.

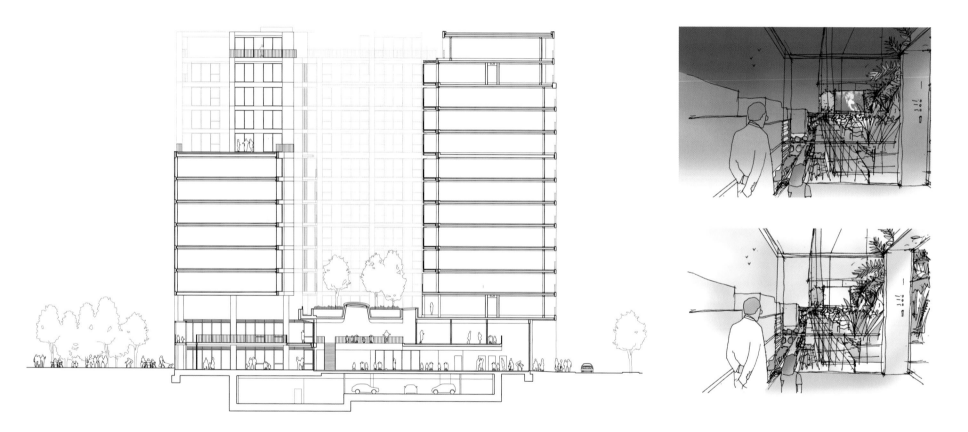

LEFT
Cross-section.

TOP RIGHT
Potential for the wintergardens to be used
for nightime events.

BOTTOM RIGHT
View from the glass lift to the rooftop
wintergardens.

the development that links through to the proposed green setting of the adjacent gas holder structures, the green fringes of Regent's Canal, a nearby Nature Reserve and a new park. The theme of planting permeates throughout the scheme from the school playground at ground level, to a rooftop wintergardens which will terminate an axial vista looking along the main approach from Handyside Street. The attraction of an extensive use of plants in a city centre is covered in "Natural Consequences".

A tartan structural grid unifies all of the different functional requirements of the building and reinforces the expression of the development as a series of towers, which provide articulation and grain to the outer facade. Above Level 9 the towers slim down to create generous roof terraces to the upper level apartments, provide further relief to the massing and to bring

in as much daylight as possible to the surrounding streets. Brick and glass are the predominant materials proposed for the street facades, creating a robust exterior that responds to the rich urban grain of the surrounding area—inset perimeter balconies provide outdoor space whilst retaining privacy. The internal garden-facing facades display a contrasting softer materiality created by the use of light coloured reconstituted concrete cladding panels, which provide a calm and light-reflecting background to the lush planting scheme proposed. The planting extends up the vertical facades which surround the garden. Described as warp and weft, the planting comprises horizontal bands of planting such as window boxes on the edges of the residents' balconies, and climbers that extend vertically around the sides of balconies, creating natural solar shading and privacy during the summer months.

TOP
Sketch view of the internal street in the school below the residential garden.

BOTTOM
Initial sketch of the residential roof garden showing warp and weft of greenery with formal vertical bands of planting by the landlord and informal horizontal planting along balconies.

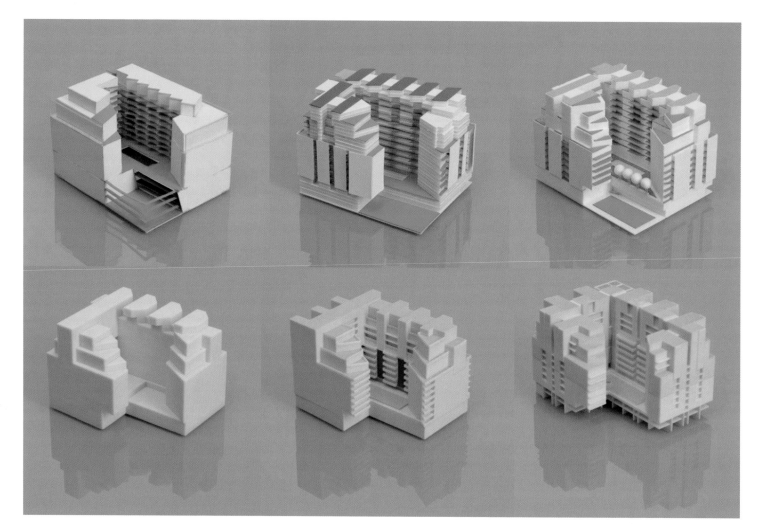

LEFT
More detailed 1:200 scale study model
in context.

RIGHT
1:1,000 scale study models initially
developed from cardboard and then using
3-D printing.

The King's Cross story is an excellent example of how the tuning in process can work to produce a focussed solution which has a sense of inevitability about it. Argent spent five years consulting with the people who would be affected by the development including businesses, residents and heritage organisations. After proposing development parameters such as land use and building height they then tested them with hypothetical designs for each site. This informed a refinement of the parameters which were subsequently agreed as part of the outline planning approval and became crystallised as a more focussed definition of the constraints and opportunities for more detailed designs for each plot. The emerging schemes for each plot have benefitted from the dialogue that Argent facilitates between the designers so they can pick up on and respond to the vibrations from their neighbours.[5]

So this shows an example of Steadman's observation that the definition of a problem to be solved is often not fixed at the outset and evolves through an iterative process taking on board feedback from the developing design. However he also acknowledges that there are some elements of an architectural brief that are "quite severe" such as geometric and topographical constraints and in this way the spatial requirements of a project and the topography of the site are fruitful areas to analyse in a linear way to define overall parameters before commencing the process of imagineering or optioneering.

This was particularly the case for Morley's first project at Lord's Cricket Ground for the Marylebone Cricket Club, known as MCC, where the brief was tightly defined. The requirement was to replace an existing facility about which many lessons had already been learnt. The Indoor School at Lord's has been covered in "Natural Consequences" and "5-D Geometry" but the process of tuning in to the competition-winning design deserves mention. Although the brief was very concise, it was through a casual conversation with some users of the existing facility that the two core priorities for the new building emerged most clearly and these were the quality of the light and the quality of the playing surface. Having found an innovative solution to the lighting, the clarity of the brief allowed the other requirements of the building to be quite precisely resolved and a comparison of the model presented to MCC at the end of the initial six week competition to the completed building shows a startling similarity.

TOP
Model of Lord's Indoor School as prepared for the initial competition.

BELOW
Photograph showing the similarity between the completed building and the initial competition model.

There are certainly occasions when the constraints of a project are so severe that the need for numerous design iterations is reduced by necessity. For example, following the completion of the Lord's Indoor School and during the construction of the adjacent headquarters building for the England and Wales Cricket Board, MCC decided to redevelop the **Lord's Shop**. This was formerly located in a converted two-storey cottage. The constrained floor area and contorted plan regularly caused extensive queuing, inconvenience to the public and lost revenue to the MCC. Following the offer of some support from the England and Wales Cricket Board chairman, Lord MacLaurin, then also chairman of Tescos, it was agreed in late 1995 to replace the existing shop with a new much larger semi-permanent building. However, to make this commercially viable it had to be completed before the first test match against India scheduled for 26 May 1996. In order to meet this demanding timescale the design had to be completed in just ten weeks with a construction period of 12 weeks and that included securing planning approval and conservation area consent for demolishing the original building. The site was also tightly

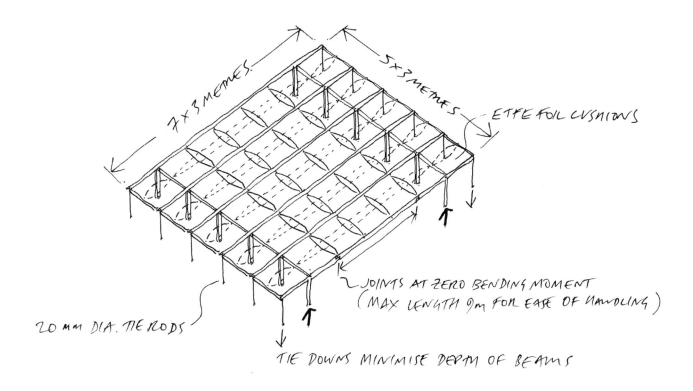

7 X 3 METRES.

5 X 3 METRES

ETFE FOIL CUSHIONS

20 MM DIA. TIE RODS

JOINTS AT ZERO BENDING MOMENT
(MAX LENGTH 9m FOR EASE OF HANDLING)

TIE DOWNS MINIMISE DEPTH OF BEAMS

constrained and the floor area had to be maximised. The context determined that key views of the building would be from the Mound Stand above and so the roof was an important fifth elevation. The tuning in process was helped because the construction was to be carried out by the existing contractor who was building the adjacent offices. The rectangular building shape was determined by extending the footprint as far as the constraints of the adjacent uses would allow. The pedestrian access and public front of the building, glimpsed through the Lord's Ground East Gates, faced west and so a generous overhang was proposed to shade the clear glazed elevation, maximising transparency and giving shelter for the crowds arriving at the shop. The idea of natural light through the roof, to create something akin to the feeling of shopping in a marquee, was a logical extension of the use of natural light adopted at the Lord's Indoor School and the adjacent offices. The use of daylight also suggested a roof which would be visually interesting. Early iterations explored a tented roof design but it was quickly established that the extreme timescales would prohibit any complicated bespoke components which would require special patterns to be made. This led to an alternative proposal which could be rapidly procured using ethylene tetrafluoroethylene, known as ETFE, foil cushions in a way that they had never been used before, spanning directly onto simple cambered steel I-beams. With this technology an articulated roof form can be simply achieved by encapsulating three rectangular layers of foil and then inflating them at a low pressure to form cushions. The solution gives a soft quality of daylight, good insulation and is visually interesting when viewed from above. The feasibility of achieving this form of construction was established by direct dialogue with the supply chain of 'producers', in this case Littlehampton Welding, who were already supplying steel for the offices next door and Vector Foil who supplied at short notice the ETFE cushions. A clear span retail area was created with very small steel I-beams by cantilevering beyond column lines at the front and back of the retail area and tieing down the overhanging lengths of beam with tension rods to reduce the bending moment in the mid-span. This gave an extraordinarily slender span to depth ratio of just 1:50.[6]

OPPOSITE LEFT
The entrance canopy provides shelter, shade and enhances structural efficiency.

OPPOSITE TOP RIGHT
Detail of ETFE roof, with the Mound Stand by Hopkins Architects in the background.

OPPOSITE BOTTOM RIGHT
View showing the naturally-lit interior.

ABOVE
Diagram of the structural principle to minimise the span to depth ratio.

TOP
View of the main entrance.

BOTTOM
Lord's Shop in the foreground with
the England and Wales Cricket Board
Headquarters behind and the Indoor
School in the background.

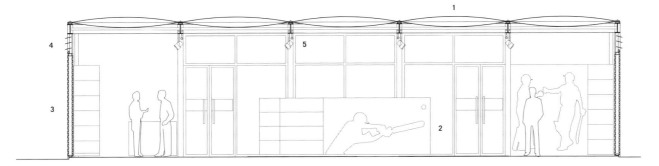

TOP
Cross-section:
1 Translucent ETFE foil cushions spanning onto 300 millimetre deep steel 'I' beams
2 Main shop
3 Sinusoidal metal cladding panels
4 Glass louvres for natural cross-ventilation
5 Track for lighting and sprinklers

BOTTOM
A spin-off from a translucent daylit building is a gentle nightime glow.

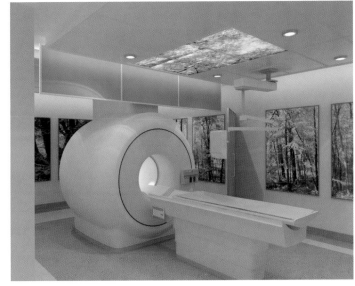

The tuning in process was also accelerated by using the expertise and resources of Tesco for fitting out the shop. However, there was some controversy about the use of natural light which was not at that time considered desirable in shops. It is notable that since then a number of supermarkets, including some Tesco stores, have deployed natural light as a way reducing energy costs and creating a more humane shopping environment.

The commercial imperative of the Lord's Shop was highlighted by the fact that, within the first season of opening, the increased revenue more than covered the construction cost of the building. In this case the definition of best "possible solution" was also informed by extreme constraints of time and cost.

When the brief is less well defined a structured process of dialogue and communication is needed to adequately tune in. For example, when designing healthcare buildings, the plethora of required space types generate a vast range of potential organisational solutions some of which are best for the patient experience, some of which are more efficient for nursing staff and some of which are inherently more flexible to accommodate evolving technologies. There is also the need to integrate healthcare buildings into their community and deliver them cost effectively.

The concept for David Morley Architects' first healthcare project for the Hospital of St John and St Elizabeth was inspired by a conversation with the Hospital Director, Stuart Twaddell, where the analogy between a hospital and an airport emerged early on. Both hospitals and airports need to encourage potentially stressed-out visitors to feel calm. They need to be designed to ease way-finding through a complicated network of spaces and there are analogies in the planning requirements of airside and landside for an airport compared to clean and dirty areas in a hospital. For this and subsequent major hospital projects the parallels with airports have been expressed by announcing the point of arrival with a welcoming canopy to provide shelter, orientation and a clear sense of legibility about the function of the building.

In order to advance detailed layouts David Morley Architects developed a form of illustrated room data sheet which allows the design team to have a focussed one-to-one dialogue with individual users concerning specific areas of the building. Easily understood three-dimensional visualisations, whether through sketches, photorealistic images or full-scale mock-ups are deployed to gather information about component parts. In this way it is possible to advance the design in specific areas whilst the overall design is still uncertain. This process

OPPOSITE
Entrance Canopy for Hospital of St John and St Elizabeth.

LEFT
Entrance Canopy for Kent Institute of Medical Science.

RIGHT
Three-dimensional room data sheet for Southmead Hospital, Bristol.

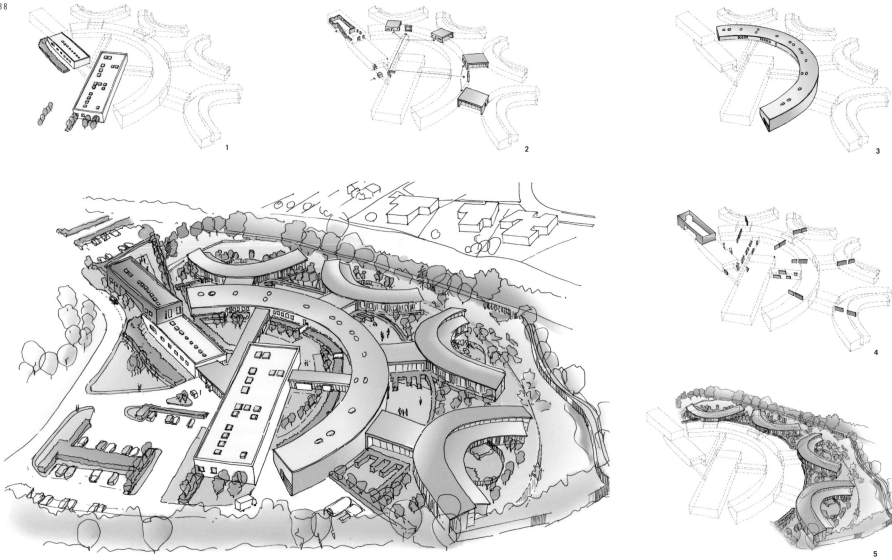

1 TO 5
Bluestone Unit Concept
1 Simple, familiar entrance buildings
2 Thresholds between key spaces marked
   by the use of natural timber
3 Crescent of communal spaces shared
   between wards
4 The way-finding is reinforced with a
   sequence of art installations
5 The smaller crescent shaped wards open
   up to the landscape beyond

LEFT
Initial sketch study for the Bluestone Unit
in Craigavon, Northern Ireland, showing
the buildings forming a hierarchy of secure
external spaces.

is similar to that proposed by Alexander where he advocates dealing with an ill-defined or very complex brief by separating out the component parts through a series of stages and establishing a preferred solution to each sub-problem as part of the journey towards solving the larger whole.

Arguably, designing for mentally ill patients is even more complex than for acute care since the architecture has even more prominence as part of the process of healing. The brief for the **Bluestone Unit** in Craigavon in Northern Ireland comprised an inpatient unit with 74 single en suite bedrooms, and a day resource centre treating male and female acute adults and older people with mental ill health, day patients and outpatients.[7]

The concept was to create a strong integration between buildings, landscape and art to exploit their combined therapeutic potential. In

plan the unit is designed in layers with the public facing areas towards the front of the building, becoming more private towards the back. The building form provides the orientation and security for visitors, residents and staff. In section the design uses high-glazed panels to provide visual connections between the interior and exterior spaces. As a mental health unit it is important to create a non-threatening environment which is sensitive to the diverse needs of people with mental illness. The entire building is single-storey, a less intimidating domestic scale which allows the buildings, rather than fences, to create a hierarchy of secure outdoor spaces. Materials were chosen for their natural, soft qualities, whilst strong colours have been used to create a lively non-clinical environment. Colour is also used to identify circulation routes, for example timber defines the public areas, from the reception desk through to the wards.

The public buildings to the front relate to the local vernacular and are white, orthogonal, definitive and familiar whilst the shapes become more organic to embrace and provide privacy for patients to the rear. Glazing is used extensively giving a strong link between the internal and external areas, with views onto the landscaped courtyards. The connection with nature is reinforced by integrated art, from a specially commissioned panel of artists, to promote a sense of wellbeing and help create engaging spaces.

In the post-occupancy evaluation the scheme achieved a National Health Service Environmental Assessment Toolkit (NEAT) Excellent rating. This project began with a client setting aspirations for a building that would help break the mould of previous mental healthcare buildings by creating a healing environment rather than just a place to be kept safe. The

ambitions are for mental health staff of the future to be considered more like life coaches than institutional carers. The whole project team were incentivised by a selection process based on partnering, whereby the quality of the process and product would determine future opportunities to work together. So the process of dialogue extended beyond completion to encompass frank post-occupancy reviews.

Some key points emerging were a marked decrease in the number of disruptive incidents and a generally less aggressive atmosphere. The contact with nature was much appreciated and important simple details were noted such as being able to hear the birds sing. Ease of supervision makes the staff less stressed and ease of access to flexible communal spaces both indoors and outdoors was seen to make a significant contribution to the sense of wellbeing.

LEFT
Sky to Earth sculpture by Alan Burke with the timber clad entrance beyond.

RIGHT
The *Mirror Trees* by Shirley McWilliam turn the normally institutional convex security mirror into a means for expressing the views and feelings of patients.

RIGHT
Circulation routes are daylit and articulated
by the timber structure. The link with the
landscape beyond is reinforced by Andrea
Spencer's glass installations on the theme of
"Harmonies with New Green and Sea Blue".

OPPOSITE
Post-occupancy feedback has confirmed
how much the contact with nature is valued.

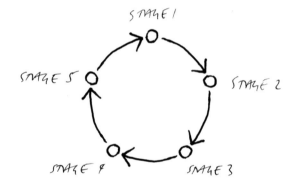

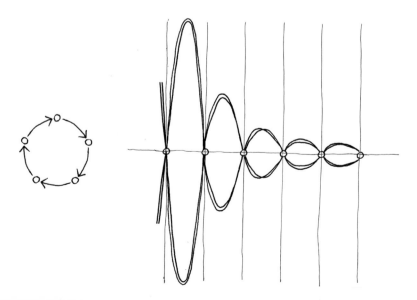

Post-occupancy evaluation and review is an essential part of the tuning in process and deserves to become more widely formalised as part of a design team's appointment. Indeed the "Soft Landings" initiative developed by the Building Services Research and Information Association (BSRIA) was set up to recognise and overcome problems beyond building handover. They have defined "Soft Landings" as meaning:

> … designers and constructors staying involved with buildings beyond practical completion. This will assist the client during the first months of operation and beyond, to help fine-tune and de-bug the systems, and ensure the occupiers understand how to control and best use their buildings.

In tune with Five by 5 is it a coincidence that BSRIA have structured their framework into five stages? They are as follows:

Stage 1: Inception and briefing—More time for constructive dialogue between the designer, constructor and client.

Stage 2: Design development and review—Brings the entire project team together to review insights from comparable projects and detail how the building will work from the point of view of the manager and individual user.

Stage 3: Pre-handover—Enables operators to spend more time on understanding interfaces and systems before occupation.

Stage 4: Initial aftercare—Continuing involvement by the client, design and building team benefiting from lessons learned and occupant satisfaction surveys.

Stage 5: Years 1–3 extended after care and Post-occupancy Evaluation—Completing the virtuous circle for future projects, to close the loop between design expectation and reality.

The reference to closing the loop suggests that the tuning in process is less of a linear progression and follows a more circular trajectory, but there is a flaw in this analogy since it suggests that the end point is the

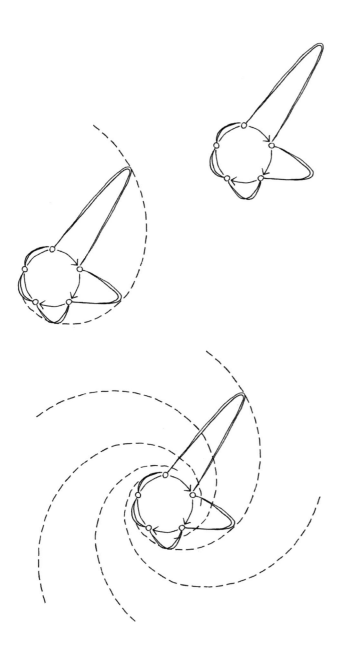

same as the start point. A closed loop virtuous circle neither takes account of the value of lessons learnt, nor the non-linear nature of the iterative process of design. However by overlaying the tuning in process diagram, described earlier in this chapter, on top of a diagram of a virtuous circle, a spiral can be generated which is a better way of articulating the design process. A spiral suggests a sense of progress towards a goal. Furthermore, since the tuning in diagram was generated by golden ratios, the spiral generated is a golden spiral as found in nature.

This links back to 5-D Geometry where this chapter started. The golden spiral represents a harmonious progression towards an increasingly focussed design solution. However, the spiral can also be seen as an equally harmonious expansion outwards, representing the signals being sent out which, when combined together, make the tuning in process possible.

1. *The Architects' Journal*, 2 June 2005.

2. The condition to build a construction training centre became a legally-binding agreement known as a "Section 106 contribution" under Section 106 (S106) of the Town and Country Planning Act 1990.

3. *Architecture Today*, Issue 199.

4. Originating from Holland the concept for a Home Zone is defined by the Institute of Highway Engineers as a street where people and vehicles share the road space on equal terms and where quality of life takes precedence over ease of traffic movement.

5. John Durham Peters in *Speaking into the air* notes how the language associated with radio is used to describe methods of communication such as "tuning in or out, being on the same wavelength, good and bad vibes, noise reduction".

6. 1:20 is frequently quoted as a typical span to depth ratio for a simply supported I-beam.

7. The Bluestone Unit was designed by David Morley Architects in collaboration with Hall Black Douglas Architects.

OPPOSITE TOP
The five stages of the "Soft Landings" post-occupancy review process.

OPPOSITE MIDDLE
The virtuous circle of "Soft Landings".

OPPOSITE BOTTOM
The "Soft Landings" virtuous circle combined with the process of "Tuning In".

TOP
The process of "Tuning In" overlaid on the "Soft Landings" virtuous circle.

MIDDLE
The overlaid processes describe a golden spiral.

BOTTOM
The refined process of "Tuning In".

The role of the architect in the creation of buildings, spaces and places is quite unlike that of any other contributor to the built environment. The everyday matters of producing designs capable of achieving planning permission, production drawings that meet regulatory standards, and of engaging with the myriad organisations and individuals who may assist or inhibit development is part of that story.

At the heart of the architect's role, however, is design—a word that does not necessarily chime with the familiar British attitude to "beauty being in the eye of the beholder". The reduction of architecture to being a matter of what something looks like is the result of a defective education system in which the verbal is prioritised over the visual. One consequence is articles about designs where hundreds of words are used to describe tiny two-dimensional images of what may not even yet exist.

In reality the way things look are the result of a series of factors or conditions which the architect needs to integrate as part of a harmonious whole, where space, volume, materials, light and so on are blended in proportions that contribute to the desired outcome.

Part of the architect's skill, by virtue of education, training and experience, is to understand the brief in all its dimensions, both literal and metaphorical: not simply how the building functions, but how it feels; what it contributes to its environment; how it will be both perceived and used. David Morley's suggestion that architecture can be thought about as five-dimensional, and the work cited as examples, are an apposite reminder of the limits of how certain aphorisms about architecture, for example 'form follows function', are inadequate as explanations and dangerous as rationales for what should be synthetic design.

Simple-minded approaches to the analysis of site and programme are eschewed in Morley's work, whether for an Oxbridge College, a sports building or pavilion in a park. Instead what you get is a clear-sighted understanding of what is doing what and why, and how the whole adds up to something greater than the sum of its parts. This means that house style is non-existent if by that one means a repeated visual look; rather, the process and underlying attitude (for example to nature) are what inform the work.

Many architects would argue, or agree, that a constituent of good design is to get different elements to do more than one thing. In Morley's case that idea is pushed so that the finished result becomes a highly integrated set of multi-functioning elements that derive from a process of discovery about site, brief, construction and materials, but always bearing in mind those other dimensional elements related to how the building feels and changes through time.

In this, the work of the practice is both clear and complex, robust yet flexible, contributing to but also drawing from its immediate environment. It is the architectural equivalent of slow cooking.

PAUL FINCH

PREVIOUS PAGES
The arched structure of the Brunel University Athletics Centre integrates a response to the volumetric requirements of indoor sport, an efficient structure, an environmental concept and a fitting gateway for the university.

OPPOSITE
The mounded earth structure of the Regent's Park Hub visually reduces the scale of the building to be like a band stand in response to John Nash's vision of buildings as ornaments in the park, but the mound also creates a viewing terrace for spectators and forms part of the environmental control strategy.

Plan of the University of Liverpool Precinct:
1 Liverpool Biosciences Centre
2 Existing refurbished laboratories
3 New Life Sciences Quad
4 Eastern Gateway to the City of Liverpool
5 Abercromby Square

The last chapter illustrated how, through a process of "Tuning In", a very broad range of ideas and viewpoints can be distilled through a structured process of dialogue and communication. The importance of "Integration" is to synthesise all of those multiple inputs so that they enrich, rather than complicate, designs. If one idea can be found that addresses many different issues this should lead to an inherently more economic and more integrated design, which does more with less. It also should make design more interesting, because an integrated idea can be appreciated in more than one way and it therefore becomes easier to satisfy the broad range of interested parties who typically engage with a project. If an idea works at several different levels, you only need to buy into one of those levels to support the idea. The phrase "designed by committee" is often used in a derogative way to suggest that "too many cooks spoil the broth" but through a process of integration the opposite can be true, a design can become deeper and more rewarding, like a simple solution to a complex problem.

The process of "Integration" works in all aspects of architecture from master planning through to fine detail. Beginning with the master plan, in

"5-D Geometry" the plan for St Hugh's College was shown to combine a concept for creating a sequence of garden spaces with an environmental idea for giving all student rooms an east or west aspect. The master plan for the P1 Development at King's Cross Central described in "Tuning In" focussed on a garden opening up to the southwest to combine good views with good sunlight and create a site for a school playground which would have the best possible adjacencies to the surrounding amenities. In both these examples there was more than one reason for the layout to be as proposed. This was also the case for the design for the **Liverpool Biosciences Centre**, completed in 2003, which involved a development of the University's master plan.

The project brought together, for the first time, all the research groups of the school on to a single site. This not only allowed the groups to interact and share knowledge and expertise, but also maximised the efficiencies of shared space and freed up existing buildings for future renovation and expansion for other University departments. The site occupies the northeast corner of the "University Precinct" and is adjacent to a major vehicle route in to the City of Liverpool which is now known

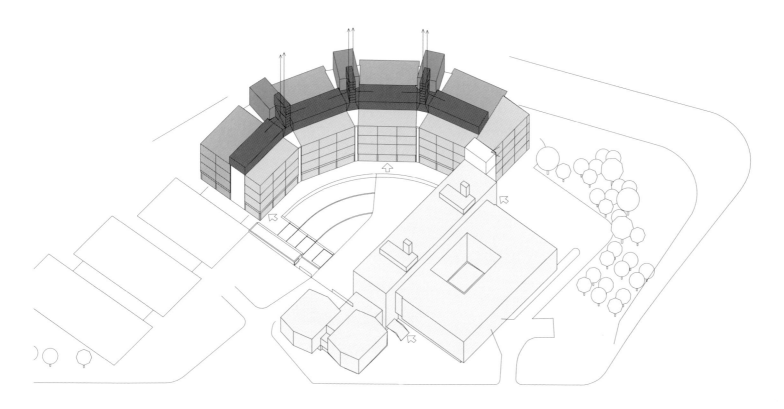

as the "Eastern Gateway". Liverpool's architecture can be characterised by its generous scale, a tradition of innovative and pioneering buildings and a landmark skyline. The elevated nature of the site and the town planning context of large surrounding buildings, offered an opportunity for developing a landmark relating to both the university and the city. Thus, the Liverpool Biosciences Centre, in conjunction with existing and planned developments of medical facilities to the north of the site reinforces the synergy between the university and the city. The University of Liverpool was laid out in accordance with the original Georgian street pattern centred around the fine central Abercromby Square which was originally to a plan by John Foster (1758–1827) and then expanded in accordance with the William Holford (1907–1975) master plan as an orthogonal 'patchwork' of buildings and green squares linked by a network of pedestrian routes. However, this clear pattern of planned spaces and buildings petered out adjacent to the Liverpool Biosciences Centre site where the layout lacked coherence and the buildings were aligned on different geometries. The existing Life Sciences Building was a nine-storey 1960s structure comprising a three-storey podium with internal courtyard and a six-storey tower above this. The tower suffered from fabric deterioration, statutory

compliance problems and structural problems, and the top five storeys were removed after the new facility was built and the existing research facilities had been decanted.

The new accommodation is arranged as a series of rectangular blocks linked by wedge-shaped support accommodation. The sum of these parts forms a crescent-shaped building which responds to the corner site and "Eastern Gateway" to the city on the outside and creates a more intimate pedestrian quad within. Although a university 'quad' is traditionally rectangular, in this case the quad is a geometric quadrant.

Mechanically ventilated and sealed laboratories face out towards the busy road to the north allowing extensive areas of glazing, giving excellent daylight with no solar gain. Naturally ventilated offices face into the south-facing courtyard which is protected from the noise and traffic fumes. Internal functions are expressed externally by large north-facing windows which optimise light to the deep plan laboratories and smaller south-facing windows for the shallower plan of the offices. The services are organised into a vertical fully accessible interstitial wall which feeds horizontally into

Liverpool Biosciences Centre functional arrangement:

- Generic research laboratories
- Plant
- Interstitial service wall and extract flues
- Academic write-up offices
- Existing refurbished teaching spaces with research tower removed.

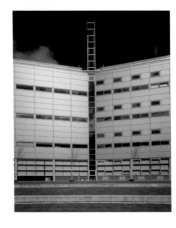

TOP LEFT
Terracotta-clad service towers separate the four bays of the quadrant shaped plan.

BOTTOM LEFT
The laboratory blocks are articulated with mini-atria below each service tower.

RIGHT
South-facing offices and write-up spaces define a Life Sciences Quad. Windows are sized to suit the shallow floor plan and facilitate natural cross ventilation.

the laboratories and vertically into the service wedges which articulate the crescent shape of the building and integrate the essential flue structures into a coherent architectural whole. The palette of finishes draws on the terracotta colours typical of Liverpool sandstone and many of the older university buildings in the form of rainscreen tiles, louvres and baguette screens, in order to articulate the different elements of the massing and roofscape. The prominent flue structures, designed to support the exhaust flue pipes from fume cupboards and safety cabinets within the building, sit at the apex of the wedge elements and provide vertical articulation to the facetted form of the new building.

This articulation is reinforced by placing vertical atria at each internal facet to provide staff break-out spaces.

Ideas that work simultaneously from the outside in and from the inside out are a second theme of "Integration". At the Lord's Indoor School, described in "Natural Consequences", the spectator facilities are arranged as a double-sided pavilion so that all of the ancillary accommodation for the building, such as changing rooms, bar, offices and classrooms, is located beneath a series of terraces which offer views internally down the nets and externally out to the adjacent Nursery Cricket Ground.

LEFT
Night view of a typical mini-atrium showing colour-coded break-out spaces at each level.

RIGHT
Up view of a typical mini-atrium with break-out balcony spaces.

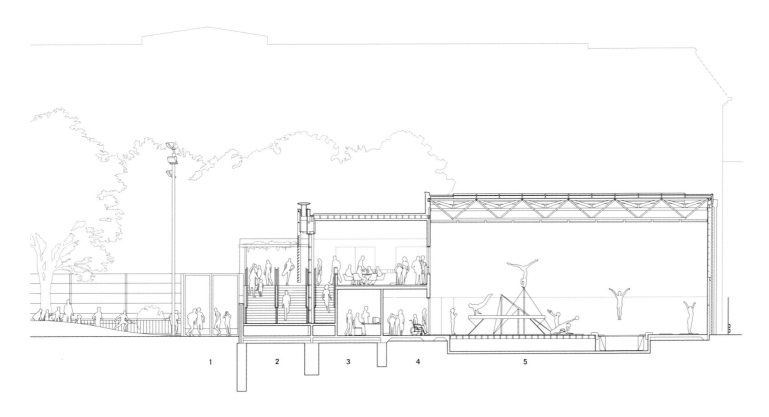

The idea of a double-sided pavilion was subsequently used at Morley's **Talacre Community Sports Centre** in Camden, London, completed in 2003. The building and adjacent park are designed to encourage participation of the whole community in sports development from the level of play and recreation through to sporting excellence by promoting good visual and physical interconnections from within the park and within the building. The UK's first purpose built three-storey high 'soft play' centre is prominently located at the entrance to unify the play functions of the park and building. Beyond that, a gymnastics hall forms the conceptual heart of the building with views in from the soft play centre and social areas through glazed screens and viewing galleries. The building aims to break down barriers to physical activities by encouraging very young children in the soft play area to eventually move to more serious and skilled activities in the spaces adjacent. The elongated plan form for this building resulted from the constrained site but led to an opportunity for all of the ancillary accommodation to take the form of a double-sided pavilion overlooking the park on the outside and the indoor sports on the other. The outward-

looking aspect of the building was designed to give passive overlooking and security to make the adjacent park feel safer. Whereas the park used to be a threatening unsecure space nick-named as Camden's "needle exchange", the newly configured gardens have now become a safe and much-loved community asset recognised with many awards.

Whereas overlooking is often a positive aspect of design there are certain ethnic groups who will only participate in sport if they have complete privacy. This normally means separate spaces with no inter-visibility but at the Talacre Community Sports Centre the internal gallery was lined with shutters which were integrated into the design to give the opportunity for privacy—a key criteria for encouraging female Muslim groups to participate. There are three halls in total: gymnastics; multi-purpose and soft play. For future flexibility the structure is generic for all halls and is engineered so that all of the main areas can operate during daylight hours without artificial light—a key principle that helps minimise the environmental impact of this building type whilst also making it a more

OPPOSITE
Site plan showing the Talacre Community Sport Centre and adjacent Talacre Gardens:
1 Entrance court
2 Double-sided pavilion
3 Soft Play Centre and Sports Halls
4 Formal play areas
5 Informal play areas

ABOVE
Cross-section through Talacre Community Sports Centre:
1 Outdoor play areas
2 Outdoor viewing terrace
3 Indoor viewing gallery and juice bar
4 Circulation
5 Gymnastics Hall

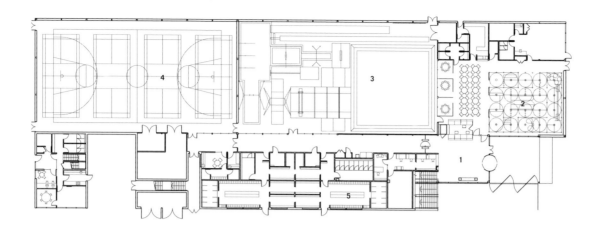

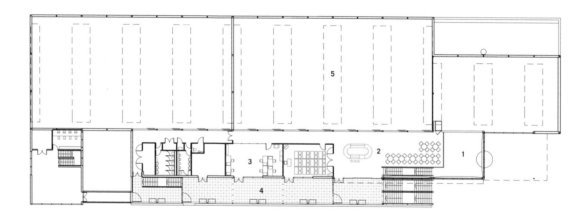

Ground floor plan:
1   Entrance
2   Soft Play Centre
3   Gymnastics Hall
4   Multi-purpose Hall
5   Changing rooms and ancillary
    accommodation

MIDDLE LEFT
First floor plan:
1   Void over entrance
2   Juice bar
3   Meeting rooms
4   Terrace
5   Rooflights above

BOTTOM LEFT
The juice bar is strategically located with
views to indoor and outdoor formal sport.

RIGHT
The internal gallery can be screened off
with sliding shutters.

enjoyable place to be in. Soon after it opened Council figures showed the centre was used by more than 10,000 people in its first seven weeks, far exceeding expectations. The Gardens have since been adopted by the local community as a much treasured asset.

The ability to accommodate different uses into one generic space is a third theme of "Integration". The benefits of this form of integration are not only to achieve better space utilisation, as was shown in "Tuning In" at The Campus, but also to support a more integrated cultural setting, as seen at Talacre. Also, in the Regent's Park Hub, described in "Natural Consequences", both the master plan and the building itself integrate sports and non-sports users alike. By making more efficient pitch and pathway layouts, it was possible to allocate more space for an ecologically rich landscape setting for strolling and picnics. Within the Hub building, the changing rooms have sliding partitions that allow three pairs of football changing rooms to be opened up to form spaces for such diverse uses as cricket tea rooms, lecture rooms or yoga studios. The idea of integrating and encouraging interaction between many different types of users, including the local community, students and elite athletes was central to the concept for the **English Institute of Sport at the University of Bath**, completed in 2004. Here, participation in sport is encouraged by promoting

strong visual links between outside and inside and within the building itself. The first step to achieve this was to find a site for new sports facilities that could link together with existing sports facilities on the campus through a single entrance to create an integrated "Sports Village". This was achieved by radically re-planning the entrance to the University and to make the University's central park a more visible focus for approaching visitors. The Institute is a centre for training elite athletes with a particular focus on athletics, swimming, tennis, netball and judo, but it's more than a place to just practice sport. The concept of the 'Institute' is to nurture the wellbeing of athletes in a fully holistic sense. The response to this objective was to focus all the facilities around a central gallery that aligned with a vista from the lake at the centre of the University, through the indoor facilities and out to the outdoor facilities and horizon beyond, symbolically linking life of the University, sport and life outside the University. The gallery was then made as the focus for the facilities common to all sports. The site is also next to an "Area of Outstanding Natural Beauty" and so it was important that the scheme respected this. The building shape echoes the barrel vaulted roof forms of the nearby Roman baths, and the Olympic sporting tradition is reflected in the external colonnade that provides a covered link between the University to the north and the community to the south.

LEFT
Adjacent to the Talacre Community Sports Centre entrance there is access to a first floor terrace which overlooks the park to give passive supervision.

RIGHT
The southwest facing reception wall is shaded externally and naturally ventilated via a roof mounted aileron.

LEFT
The west-facing colonnade mediates between the scale of the sports halls and the parkland setting whilst also providing shade and shelter for visitors arriving from either the north or south.

RIGHT
View of the University of Bath showing the context for the English Institute of Sport.

LEFT
The central gallery offers views down into the strength and conditioning suite and provides a focus for all sports users whether they be elite athletes, students or from the local community.

RIGHT
The elliptical columns of the colonnade exploit the properties of steel with massive 18 metre spans expressing muscularity and athleticism. The walls are made from terracotta blockwork to reflect the colour of Bath stone.

TOP
View of the Tennis Hall showing the integration of structure, envelope, natural light, artificial light, heating and netting trackways.

BOTTOM
Summary of concept
1 Colonnade, entrance, shelter and sun shade combine together to mediate the scale of the large sports halls with the adjacent park
2 New Sports Halls
3 Existing Sports Halls
4 Central Gallery
5 External Viewing Terrace forms roof to the 140 metre sprint track below

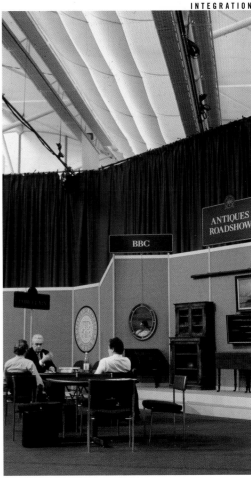

The entrance to the gallery is at first floor level and in addition to the vista at either end there are views into the sport activities on either side. Key to the design of this building is the recognition that sports training no longer comprises purely practicing a particular sport. It is now much more about an athlete's whole wellbeing and this includes diet, sports medicine, psychology and most importantly strength and conditioning. So the concept for this Institute was to place these facilities, which are common to all athletes, at the heart of the building in a gallery which would link all of the sports specific halls. In this way athletes in tennis, judo, fencing, swimming, badminton, netball, and modern pentathlon can all share ideas and techniques. The elite facilities are also opened up to the public so that students and local residents can work-out next to Olympic champions and furthermore, everyone who comes into the building can see that happening because it is open to view from the main entrance.

The process of "Integration" flows through the whole of the design and in particular to the integration of the structure with the environmental control systems for the building. For example, in the tennis hall, triangular section trusses support rooflights above with lights, nets and radiant heaters below without any need for secondary structure, the building grid reconciles the sizes needed for sport with the optimum spans of liner trays and cladding panels creating an uncluttered soffit as an ideal backdrop. The retaining wall is also a practice wall and a viewing gallery between the courts is made from a structure which also holds the roof up, provides the cross-bracing and conceals cameras and analysis rooms below.

This is the fourth theme to "Integration" and is well illustrated in sports architecture where there are many opportunities for the integration of clearly defined functional and dimensional constraints with structural and environmental systems. For example, the rooflight design at the Lord's Indoor School, illustrated in "Natural Consequences", generated a structure which spanned the length of the building and was thus able to support nets and lights without the need for any secondary structure. In addition, as a consequence of having removed the need for any columns along the side of the building, this meant that the side walls could be opened up in warm weather to allow generous natural ventilation but also provide access for lorries to drive straight into the building to increase the flexibility to set up for special events. Furthermore, since an underground railway passes below the side wall of the building, considerable savings were made by designing out the need for any special foundations.

LEFT
Removing primary structure from the edge of the Lord's Indoor School enabled the side walls to be designed to open up. It also greatly simplified the foundation details since there are railway tunnels close to the surface immediately adjacent to this side of the building. The openable side panels guarantee that on the hottest of summer days the internal environment can be generously cross-ventilated and a fresh air quality can be maintained. The large side openings also help minimise down time for equipping the hall for special events.

RIGHT
The cricket nets can be quickly converted to other uses such as this Antiques Roadshow.

RIGHT
Site Plan of the Brunel University Athletics
Centre:
1 Athletics Hall
2 Badminton, Netball and Basketball Hall
3 Pedestrian Mall
4 Existing Sports Centre
5 Student residences

OPPOSITE TOP
The Netball Hall uses the same structural
system but is lit from the end walls to avoid
overhead glare.

OPPOSITE BOTTOM
The Athletics Hall roof integrates structure,
daylight, ventilation, artificial light and an
efficient cladding envelope.

David Morley Architects completed another 'English Institute of Sport' building at Brunel University in 2005. **The Brunel University Indoor Athletics Centre** facilities are for indoor training of athletics, netball and badminton, and they are sited to create a gateway into the main pedestrian mall through the campus. Everyone passing through the gateway gets a view into the main athletics hall through low level glazing and high level openable transparent ETFE foil panels. The hyperbolic cosine arch form of the structure is derived from the most efficient span across the height constraints of sprint and hurdles at the perimeters which both require four and a half metres clear height and pole jump at the centre point which requires nine metres. At the crown of the arch is a continuous rooflight which gives an even level of natural illumination along the entire 140 metre length of the building and gives the hyperbolic cosine roof form an additional function as a giant light reflector. Each arch is made of a simple steel tube and is spaced apart from the next to optimise the span of roof liner trays that also provide stiffness eliminating the need for cross-bracing. This gives a very cost effective envelope since there is minimal external wall. At low level at the perimeter sliding glazed doors give views in and out and provide ventilation inlets. Daylight is from above and extracted air is allowed to collect naturally at high level and is simply ventilated through openable panels at either end of the hall. A pair of wishbone like struts brings the loads of two arches down to one simple foundation. This configuration reduces foundation costs and also eliminates the need for any longitudinal cross-bracing. The design is stripped back and minimal to hit stringent budget constraints but by getting each element of the building to do more than one thing there is still scope for innovation and surprise.

LEFT
The wishbone supports to each pair
of arches eliminate the need for any
longditudinal cross-bracing and halve
the number of foundations.

RIGHT
A central ETFE foil giant opening window
provides natural ventilation at either end
of each hall.

In this way, the scope for "Integration" extends right through to the finer detail of a building. The concept of the Isis Education Centre, described in "Natural Consequences", being inspired by trees, linked a philosophical idea about learning under a tree with an environmental idea about using trees to make buildings as a means of reducing carbon emissions through to a series of details that make best use of the properties of timber such as the steel connections which transfer load to the outer rings of the long pole timber constructions, the timber shingle cladding and the recycled paper insulation. At the Maplethorpe Building at St Hugh's College the window design combined thinking about daylight within the building but was also part of an elevational strategy which would break down the scale of the building in sympathy with its historical context. The exposed concrete colonnade at ground level was specified to use recycled blast furnace aggregate for two reasons. First to increase the amount of recycled materials in the building and second, because the recycled aggregate gives the concrete a yellowish hue which is similar to the colour of the stone used in the adjacent historic buildings. The Maplethorpe Building was the first building in Oxford to use terracotta cladding for the facade. The pinkish red panels were specially made in traditional kilns which gave each unit a slightly different colour and reinforced the comparison with the colour variations of the adjacent older brick buildings. The use of terracotta will be given additional relevance in the next phase of development at St Hugh's College to be known as the **Dickson Poon China Centre**. This building is conceived as pivotal within the grounds and will finally re-configure the College buildings and gardens into a coherent overall master plan. The second phase was

LEFT
The main entrance to the University passes between the sports halls where there are glimpsed views of the activities within.

RIGHT
Initial master plan for St Hugh's College showing links to the city centre in the background.

TOP
The south facing Dickson Poon China
Centre is clad with terracotta louvres. The
end elevation of the Maplethorpe Building
is on the left with the Middle Garden and
Library beyond.

BOTTOM
North elevation of the China Centre
showing the bay window overlooking
the Middle Garden.

originally planned to integrate communal and residential facilities but the amended plans now maximise the potential for new communal, academic and residential facilities, with some new accommodation to house the University's China Studies Centre. The building is arranged as a series of three linked pavilions to break down the scale and relate to the surrounding College and residential buildings. The first pavilion lies on the axis of the existing Library and Middle Garden to help define this as a key focal point of the College. On the south side the first pavilion also aligns with the entrance to the China Centre. Within the building the communal shared spaces are arranged at ground floor and basement level and at the upper levels where they can exploit the

views out across the Middle Garden. This arrangement is reinforced by a circulation rotunda which extends upwards to form a lantern bringing in daylight and articulating the roof profile. The China Centre accommodation is organised as a simple rectilinear block on the south side of the rotunda and opens onto a sunken linear courtyard. The residential accommodation is arranged over three levels with views out to the surrounding garden spaces. The overall scale of the building respects the heights of the surrounding College Buildings which are generally three and four storeys high. Each elevation has been developed to respond to the orientation to the sun and the constraints and opportunities of the site.

Precast concrete colonnade at the
Maplethorpe Building.

The east and west elevations follow the pattern set by the Maplethorpe Building both in terms of the five-bay colonnade at ground floor level and the scale and rhythm of the residential upper floors. The precast concrete columns, terracotta cladding, reconstituted stone panels cladding the structure to the upper floors and timber windows all adopt the same materials palette. The timber windows have been arranged as full-height fixed windows with an adjacent timber ventilation panel to give secure but generous natural ventilation. A small desk window is integrated into the terracotta cladding to a similar detail adopted for the Maplethorpe Building.

The north elevation is arranged as three linked pavilions. Running from west to east, the first pavilion lies on the axis of the Library. The upper levels are treated as a large bay window overlooking the Middle Garden and echoing the form of the Library frontage opposite. The northerly orientation allows extensive glass areas to be incorporated without creating problems of solar gain. The bay window will allow the internal spaces to take maximum benefit of views out to the garden. The second and third pavilions accommodate flexible space at the upper levels which is planned initially as bedrooms and meeting rooms. The elevations are treated with the same palette as the west elevation but with full and half bay windows which echo the theme of the first pavilion but with a more residential scale. Bay windows are considered appropriate for this north-facing elevation for several reasons: in general north-facing rooms are devoid of sunlight but the bay window gives an opportunity for some sunlight in the early morning and late evening; the north-facing frontage will also be enlivened by reflections from different parts of the sky from the angled glass of the bay windows and there is a strong precedent for bay windows in both the older College buildings and the Victorian houses within the College Grounds. At ground level a connecting colonnade provides covered access to the residential stair towers which are expressed externally. The restaurant and social spaces open out through a glazed screen to a terrace overlooking the garden.

Like the north elevation, the south elevation is arranged as three linked pavilions, in this case accommodating the China Centre. Each pavilion has an overhanging roof to give shade. The roof form follows the profile of the Maplethorpe Building south elevation and makes a subtle reference to a Chinese pagoda roof. Running from west to east, the first pavilion lies on the axis of the Library and is set back to create a generous canopy portico above the China Centre entrance. The facade incorporates a two storey

LEFT
The oak-clad central circulation rotunda
links all of the facilities and integrates
the Chinese Studies facilities with College
conference uses.

RIGHT
View of the sunken court with the main
circulation rotunda expressed like a Buddha
within a glazed enclosure.

high panel of natural stone in which the name of the building will be
engraved. The second and third pavilions incorporate full-height windows
to maximise the penetration of natural light and are interspersed with
solid reconstituted stone panels and timber ventilation panels. In order
to mitigate the effects of solar gain in warmer months, external louvres
are proposed to be suspended from the overhanging roof. The louvres
are made from terracotta in metal frames to help unify this elevation
with the remaining building palette. The pattern of the louvres refers to
the rhythms seen in Chinese hexagrams and the use of terracotta also
suggests a reference to China.

These examples show how "Integration" can be seen to work in five
distinct ways: first, at the level of master planning; second, by designing
simultaneously from the inside out and from the outside in; third, by
creating spaces which are flexible enough to encourage both cultural and

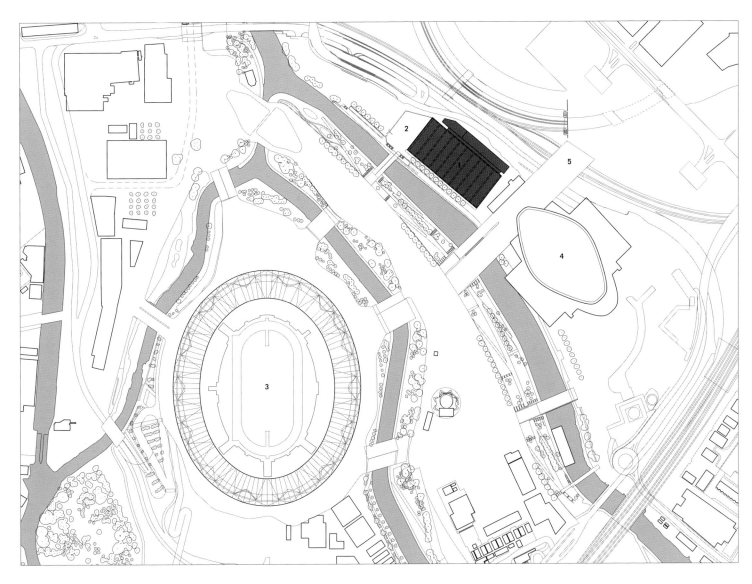

physical integration of different uses; fourth, by integrating the building fabric with the structure and environmental control strategy and finally in the fine detail and selection of materials.

"Integration" can also be seen to underlie each of the themes covered in previous chapters. Every project begins with the need to make a difference and this can happen by evolution, where integration happens by improving on existing models or by revolution, where technological advances or plain inventiveness generate new combinations of ideas. "Natural Consequences" is a way of integrating designs in accordance with all of the elements of nature to respond to the needs of society and produce architecture that is relaxed and unaffected. "5-D geometry" gives the tools to progressively integrate vision, analysis, appraisal, visualisations, a dynamic context of form, sound and time into designs which have a fifth dimension, creating an emotional or spiritual response. "Tuning In"

ensures that by initially thinking broadly, with no pre-conceptions, design solutions tightly focussed on the needs of society can emerge through a rigorous process which allows multiple inputs to be distilled—leading to "Integration", whereby each part of a design fulfils more than one function, an inherently economic approach but also one that can be enjoyed from many different viewpoints.

By using a process of integration, any one of the 25 projects featured in this book could have been illustrated in any of the five chapters because each project has integrated ideas that work in the five different ways that have been discussed. For example, **London 2012 Water Polo Arena** combines evolution with revolution. It literally uses pre-cycled components that already existed in the supply chain but uses them in a completely new way—no-one has ever designed a purpose built Water Polo Venue for a major event such as this and the use of materials such as the pthalate-

Site plan showing the London 2012 Water Polo Venue in the context of the other legacy venues and temporary structures:
1 Water Polo Venue
2 Entrance plaza
3 Olympic Stadium
4 Aquatics Centre with temporary side extensions
5 Entrance to the Olympic Park

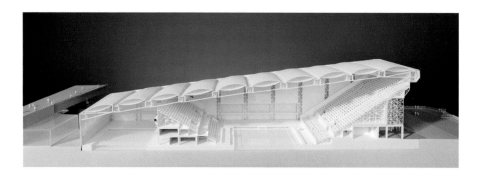

TOP
Model of the London 2012 Water Polo Venue showing the integration of function, structure, services and envelope.

BOTTOM
The London 2012 Water Polo Venue in use.

OPPOSITE
Integration leading to a focussed outcome.

free inflatable PVC roof cushions breaks new ground. Water Polo can also be seen as a "Natural Consequence". The building is designed as a re-useable kit of parts so that the resources of nature are preserved as far as possible and its form allows the majority of the building to be naturally ventilated. The shape evolved using the principles of "5-D Geometry". In 1-D, a concept for the venue to become part of two triumvirates first in a support role to the two adjacent legacy venues and second in a leading role with the temporary structures; the response to the sightlines were refined in the 2-D cross-section which is strongly expressed on the outside; the double curvature of the inflatable roof and the scalloped wall panels were sculpted in 3-D; the animation, people movement, and changing appearance in different lighting conditions over time are developed in 4-D and emphasised by a dynamic lighting system which reinforces the expression of the building as a huge splash generated by the diving figure represented by Zaha Hadid's adjacent Aquatics Centre leading to the fifth dimension where the building has a spirit beyond its functionality. The underlying golden section in the seating rake is not forced but is a natural outcome of safety regulations and available components. The process of "Tuning In" brought together a very simple solution from the multiple inputs of over 30 different consultant disciplines and the same number again of stakeholders. The product of that process was a building that, in use, has proved to work extremely well but most significantly has inspired the building users to comment that it is a building with "real soul and personality". The process of "Integration" with Water Polo began by developing a master plan where the asymmetric linear organisation for the building would not just give optimum sightlines and a simpler structure—restricting the spans to 50 metres so that they could be made from existing truss components—but also in the way it would drastically simplify people flows on the congested site bringing the majority of spectators in to the venue from a plaza adjacent to the main entrance bridge. "Integration" can be seen in the truss structures which are also lighting gantries and access walkways, all assembled at ground level and with the inflatable air cushions which give both structural support and insulation to prevent condensation.

What has emerged is that all of the chapters in this book are closely interrelated. An idea that evolves from past experience is likely to lead to a "Natural Consequence", "5-D Geometry" gives the tools for invention, evolution and revolution and "Tuning In" is the means by which to focus those inputs on to society's needs. A link between "Natural Consequences" and "5-D Geometry" can be found with underlying golden proportions, as found in nature, facilitated by the special qualities of the number five. Designs will become a "Natural Consequences" if a proper process of "Tuning In" has been followed and the process of "Tuning In" is what channels the potential of "5-D Geometry" towards a useful product.

This five way interrelationship between the subject of each chapter can be simply represented by a pentagon with all points joined together, noting that the geometry of a pentagon makes the relationships 'golden' and harmonious. However, each chapter has included five sub-topics and so a more complete picture of how they interrelate can be found by overlaying the chapter headings and sub-topics on the diagram of the "Tuning In" process. This gives an illustration of design seen as an iterative process which integrates all of the issues covered in this book into a focussed outcome which has the clarity and strength targeted by the theme of Five by 5, aiming for a signal that has excellent strength and perfect clarity—the most understandable signal possible.

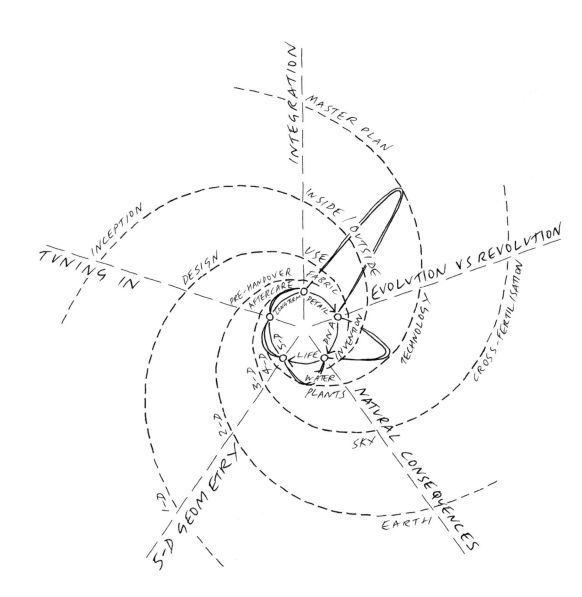

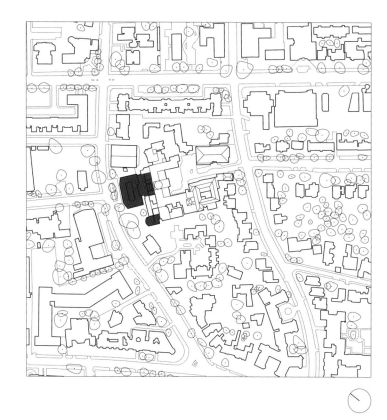

F I V E B Y 5
P R O J E C T S

HOSPITAL OF ST JOHN AND ST ELIZABETH
Completed: 1991
Client: Hospital of St John and St Elizabeth
Structural Engineer: Ove Arup and Partners
Services Engineer: Ove Arup and Partners
Quantity Surveyor: Davis Langdon and Everest
Contractor: Wates Construction (London) Ltd

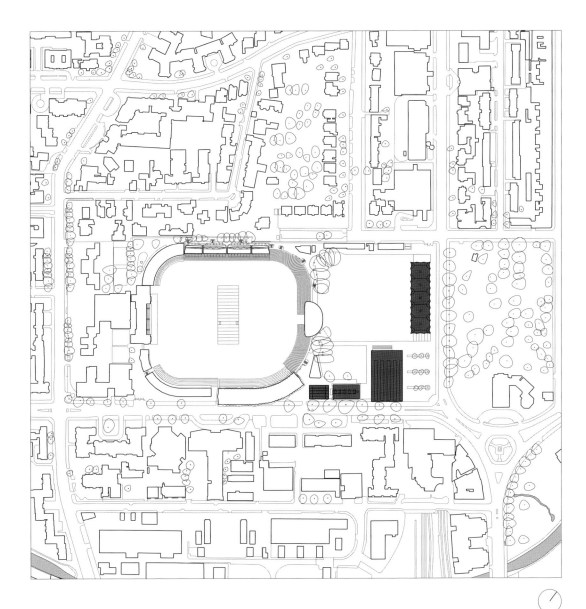

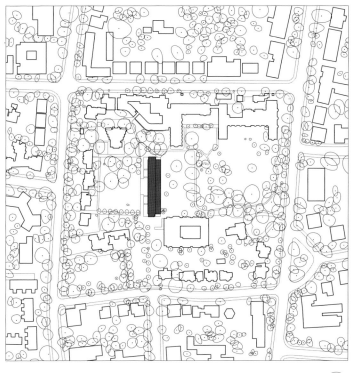

INDOOR CRICKET SCHOOL, LORD'S
Completed: 1995
Client: Marylebone Cricket Club
Structural Engineer: Price and Myers
Services Engineer: Max Fordham and Partners
Quantity Surveyor: Davis Langdon and Everest
Contractor: Wates Construction (London) Ltd

ECB HEADQUARTERS
Completed: 1996
Client: Marylebone Cricket Club
Structural Engineer: Price and Myers
Services Engineer: Max Fordham
and Partners
Quantity Surveyor: Davis Langdon and Everest
Contractor: Tolent Construction

LORD'S SHOP
Completed: 1997
Client: Marylebone Cricket Club
Structural Engineer: Price and Myers
Services Engineer: Max Fordham and Partners
Quantity Surveyor: Davis Langdon and Everest
Contractor: Tolent Construction

NURSERY PAVILION, LORD'S
Completed: 1999
Client: Marylebone Cricket Club
Structural Engineer: Atelier One
Services Engineer: Max Fordham and Partners
Quantity Surveyor: Gleeds
International Consultants
Contractor: Henry Boot Construction

**THE MAPLETHORPE BUILDING,
ST HUGH'S COLLEGE**
Completed: 2000
Client: St Hugh's College
Structural Engineer: Ove Arup and Partners
Services Engineer: Ove Arup and Partners
Quantity Surveyor: Gleeds Quantity Surveyor
Landscape Architect: Jane Fearnley Whittingstall
Contractor: Jarvis Construction Ltd

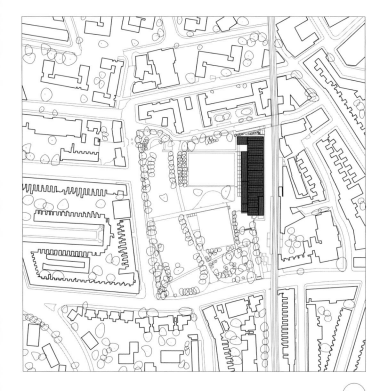

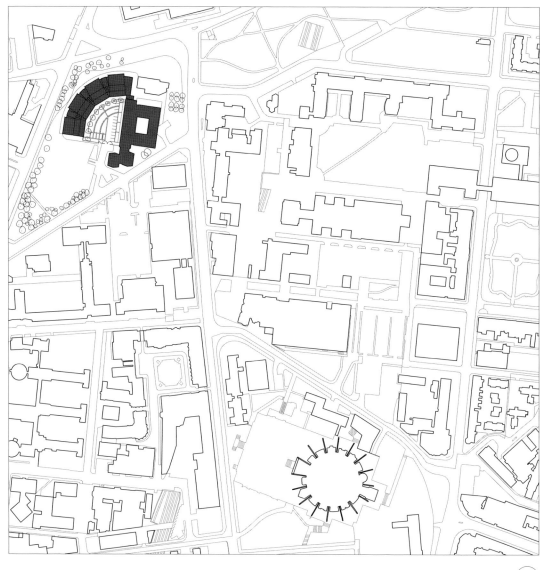

TALACRE
Completed: 2003
Client: London Borough of Camden
Structural Engineer: Price and Myers
Services Engineer: Max Fordham and Partners
Quantity Surveyor: Davis Langdon and Everest
Landscape Architect: Livingstone Eyre
Contractor: Bickerton Construction Ltd
and Leadbitter Construction

THE LIVERPOOL BIOSCIENCES CENTRE
Completed: 2003
Client: The University of Liverpool
Structural Engineer: Ove Arup and Partners
Services Engineer: Building Design Partnership
Quantity Surveyor: Tweeds
Landscape Architect: Cass Associates
Contractor: HBG Construction North West Ltd

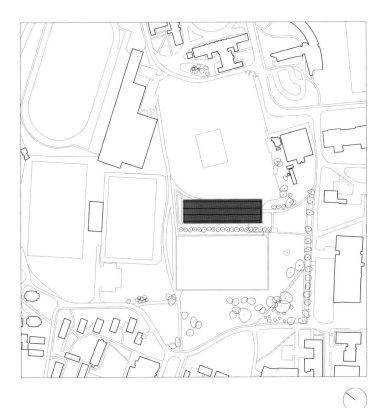

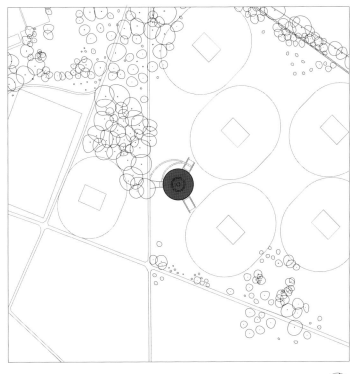

NATIONAL CRICKET ACADEMY
LOUGHBOROUGH
Completed: 2003
Client: Loughborough University
Structural Engineer: Price and Myers
Services Engineer: Max Fordham LLP
Quantity Surveyor: EC Harris
Contractor: Shepherd Construction

THE HUB, REGENT'S PARK
Completed: 2003
Client: Royal Parks Agency
Structural Engineer: Price and Myers
Services Engineer: Max Fordham LLP
Quantity Surveyor: Currie and Brown
Landscape Architect: Colvin and Moggeridge
Contractor: William Verry Ltd

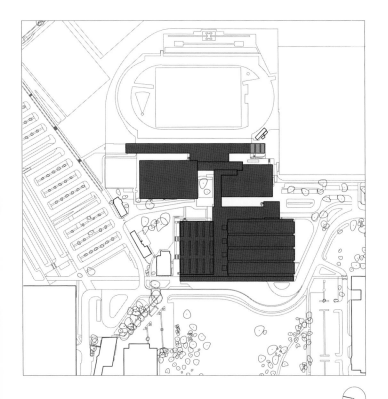

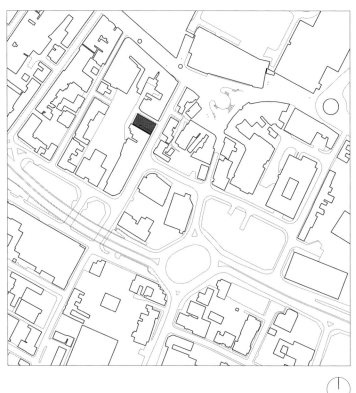

ENGLISH INSTITUTE OF SPORT
Completed: 2004
Client: University of Bath
Structural Engineer: Buro Happold
Services Engineer: Max Fordham and Partners
Quantity Surveyor: Davis Langdon and Everest
Landscape Architect: Grant Associates
Contractor: Bovis Lend Lease

LUTON WALK-IN CENTRE
Completed: 2004
Client: Luton Primary Care Trust NHS
Structural Engineer: Price and Myers
Services Engineer: Jenks Associates
Quantity Surveyor: Davis Langdonand Everest
Contractor: Crispin and Borst Ltd

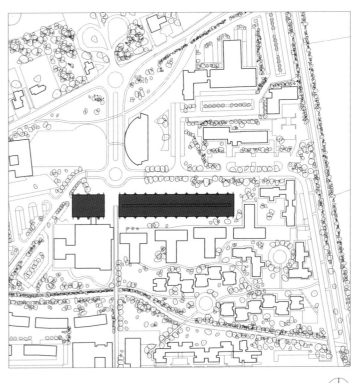

THE CAMPUS, LOCKING CASTLE
Completed: 2004
Client: North Somerset Council
Structural Engineer: Price and Myers
Services Engineer: Max Fordham LLP
Quantity Surveyor: Dickson-Powell Partnership
Landscape Architect: Livingstone Eyre
Contractor: Kier Western

**INDOOR ATHLETICS CENTRE,
BRUNEL UNIVERSITY**
Completed: 2005
Client: Brunel University
Structural Engineer: SKM Anthony Hunts
Services Engineer: Hannan and Associates
Quantity Surveyor: Hand Deere and Cox
Contractor: Galliford Try

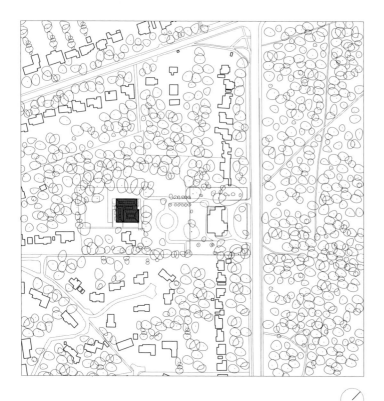

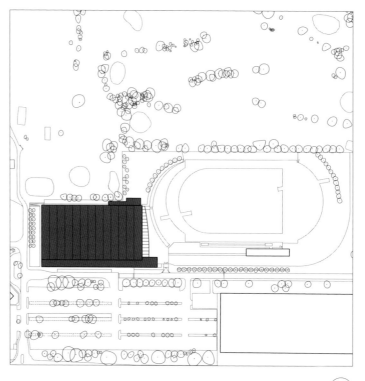

CENTRE FOR TWO ST JAMES
Completed: 2006
Client: Parish of St James, Gerrards Cross with
St James, Fulmer
Structural Engineer: Jane Wernick
Associates Ltd
Services Engineer: Max Fordham and Partners
Quantity Surveyor: Davis Langdon and Everest
Landscape Architect: Edward Hutchison
Contractor: Durtnell

LEE VALLEY ATHLETICS CENTRE
Completed: 2007
Client: Lee Valley Regional Park Authority
Structural Engineer: Buro Happold
Services Engineer: Max Fordham LLP
Quantity Surveyor: EC Harris
Landscape Architect: Livingstone Eyre
Contractor: Shepherd Construction Ltd

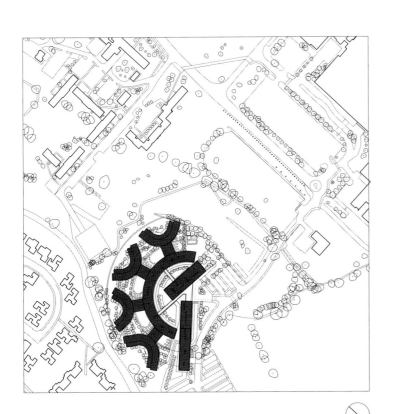

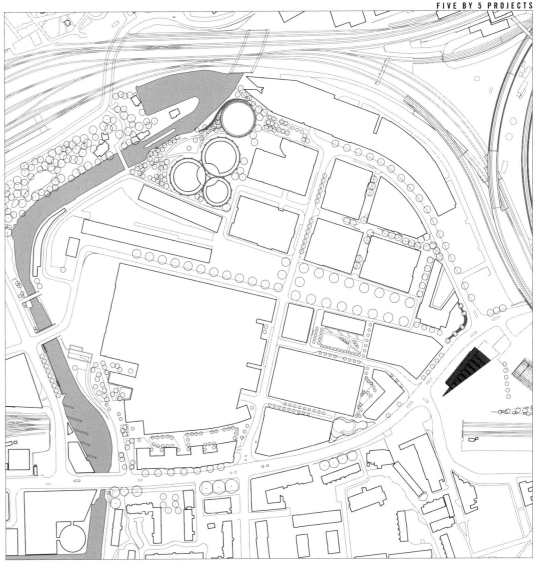

THE BLUESTONE UNIT, CRAIGAVON
Completed: 2008
Client: Craigavon and Banbridge Community
HSS Trust
Structural Engineer: Buro Happold Ltd
Services Engineer: Buro Happold Ltd
Quantity Surveyor: WH Stephens
Contractor: Heron Brothers Ltd

KING'S CROSS CONSTRUCTION
SKILLS CENTRE
Completed: 2008
Client: Argent Group PLC
Structural Engineer: TPS Consult
Services Engineer: Carillion
Quantity Surveyor: Carillion
Contractor: Carillion

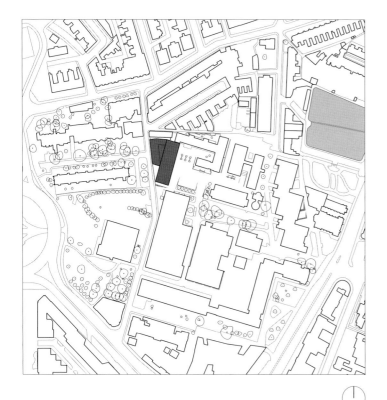

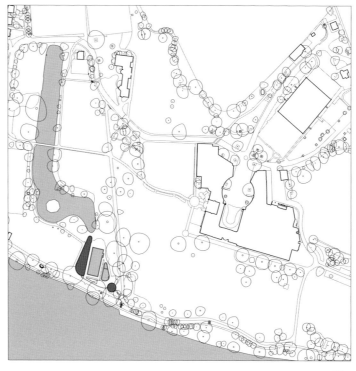

THE ROLLE BUILDING,
UNIVERSITY OF PLYMOUTH
Completed: 2008
Client: University Partnerships Programme
Structural Engineer:
Airey and Coles Consulting
Services Engineer: Max Fordham LLP
Contractor: Cowlin Construction

THE HURLINGHAM CLUB OUTDOOR POOL
Completed: 2011
Client: The Hurlingham Club
Structural Engineer: Scott White and
Hookins / Price and Myers
Services Engineer: Hoare Lea
Quantity Surveyor: Philip Uren and Co
Landscape Architect: Lucy Huntington
Garden Design
Contractor: B&K Building Services Ltd

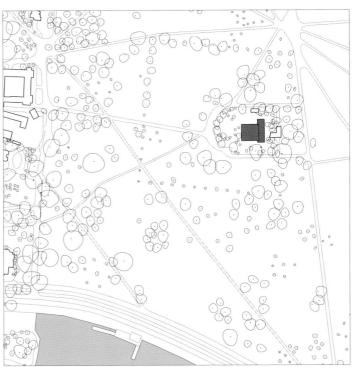

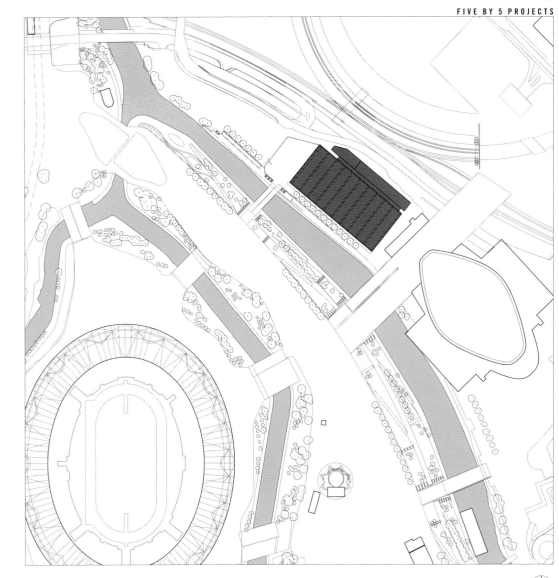

**THE ISIS EDUCATION CENTRE
AT THE LOOKOUT**
Completed: 2011
Client: The Royal Parks
/ The Royal Parks Foundation
Delivery Architect: Pellings
Structural Engineer: Price and Myers
Services Engineer: Max Fordham LLP
Quantity Surveyor: Rider Levett Bucknall
Landscape Architect: The Landscape Agency
Contractor: Fairhurst Ward Abbotts

LONDON 2012 WATER POLO ARENA
Completed: 2012
Client: Olympic Delivery Authority
Structural Engineer: Buro Happold
Services Engineer: Max Fordham LLP
Main Contractor: CLM

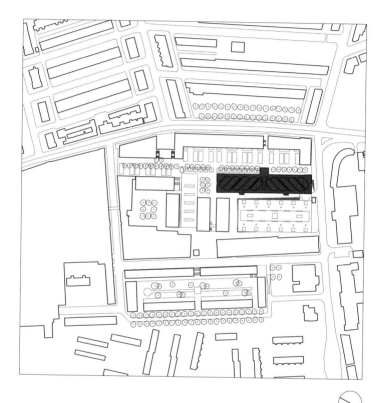

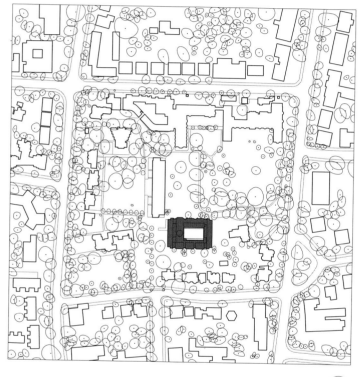

VELVET MILL, LISTER MILLS
Completion due: 2013
Client: Urban Splash
Structural Engineer: Price and Myers / ARUP
Services Engineer: WSP
Quantity Surveyor: Simon Fenton Partnership
Contractor: Urban Splash Build

THE DICKSON POON CHINA CENTRE
Completion due: 2014
Client: St Hugh's College
Structural Engineer: AKS Ward
Services Engineer: CBG Consultants
Quantity Surveyor: Davis Langdon
Landscape Architect: Land Use Consultants
Contractor: Galliford Try

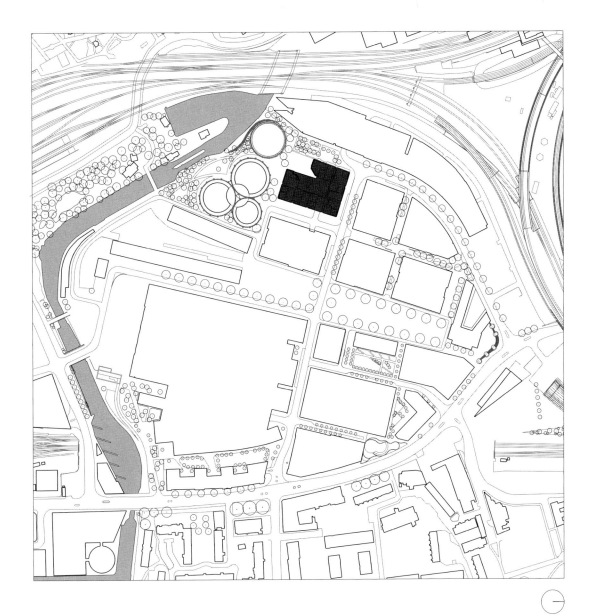

P1, KING'S CROSS CENTRAL
Completion due: 2014
Client: Argent Group PLC
Structural Engineer: Ramboll
Services Engineer: AECOM
Quantity Surveyor: Davis Langdon LLP
Contractor: Kier Build

PEOPLE

A
Naomi Ablevioch
Andrew Allsop
Claire Appleby
Marina Aragona
Helen Arvanitakis
Katie Atkinson
Ian Aw

B
Brett Baillie
Tessa Ball
Adrian Banks
Stephen Barrett
Jhanvi Bhatt
Graham Bowler
Isabel Branco
Maria Brewster
Philip Brueggemann
Mark Bunting
Ruth Butler

C
Piers Carlisle

Laura Carnell
Ulrich Centmayer
Naomi Chamberlain
Vivian Chan
Kynson Chang
Lee Chi Song
Michael Cieply
Belina Clapperton
Darren Clements
James Clunis
Mary Comerford
Catherine Compton
Paul Conway
Matt Cousins
Olivia Crawford
Anne Creola
Peter Crompton
Charlotte Crossman
Timothy Crum
Agnieszka Czapiewska

D
Mark Davies
Helen Davis

Tim Denis
Matt Dyer

E
Nancy Elgarf
Juliet Erridge
James Errington

F
Eleanor Fawcett
Michael Friel

G
Joanna Gardiner
Aris Georigiadis
Joanna Glasin
Clive Gray
Matthew Gray
Paul Gray

H
Chris Hay
Martin Hay
Marianne Heaslip

Oliver Hessian
Vincent Hewitt
Mark Homes

I

Tony Ip

J

Helen James
Alan Jones
Jennifer Juritz

K

Despoina Kapodistria
Robert Klascha
Daniel Kownacki
Jed Kritzinger
Mann Kumar
Pip Kyriacou

L

Harsh Ladd
Jen Lamont
Melanie Lamont

Richard Lawler
Youngseok Lee
Effi Leitao
Wendy Lewell
David Lewis
Philip Lyons

M

Laura MacDonald
Stuart Mackay
Nicky Margolis
Kristian Marjoram
Richard Markland
David Mathius
Andrew Metcalfe
Pengpeng Miao
Camilla Morley
David Morley
Tracy Moseley
Simone Mueller
Andy Mytom

N

Meera Nallanathan

Koichi Nogawa

P

Bobby Pang
Darren Park
Krupal Patel
Gavin Pearce
Ed Peter
Harry Philips
James Philips
Caroline Pinheiro
Matheus Pinho
Victoria Platt
Radhika Ponniah
Liam Powell
David Preece

Q

Karol Quinn

R

Ben Rees
Victoria Ridgwell
Fernanda Rivero

Chris Roberts
Kristi Rogers
Hugh Ryan

S

Danielle Schneider
King Shun
Adiane Sibitzky
Maria Smith
Richard Smith
Chi Son Lei
Suzanne Stolper
Marissa Storey
Lukasz Szafarewicz

T

Danielle Tinero
Cuong Tran-Viet
Gary Treacy
John Trenaman
Caroline Turner
Angela Tyrrell

U

Chinedu Umenyilora

V

William Valderrama
Evelyn Van Veen
Chiara Vittucci
Dan Voak
Maria Vrdoljak

W

Timothy Waines
Louisa Wan
Vincent Wan
Hongtao Wei
Jaroslaw Wieczorkiewicz
Timothy Williams
Kellie Wills
Jonathan Wilson
Mark Wilson
Karen Wong
Alastair Wood
Rhian Woods
Kim Wright
Andy Wyatt

C O N T R I B U T O R S

PETER COOK

Sir Peter Cook graduated from the AA and has been Director of the Institute of Contemporary Arts, Dean of Architecture at the Staedelschule, Frankfurt, Chair of Architecture at the Bartlett School of UCL and is Royal Academy of Arts Professor of Architecture. As a member of Archigram he was awarded the Royal Gold Medal of the RIBA and was knighted in 2007.

PAUL FINCH

Paul Finch is Chairman of Design Council Cabe (Commission for Architecture and the Built Environment), and Deputy Chairman of the Design Council itself. He is Director of the World Architecture Festival and Editorial Director of *The Architectural Review* and *The Architects' Journal*. Born London, 1949. History degree, Selwyn College, Cambridge. Deputy Editor, *Estates Times*, 1976–1983. Editor, *Building Design*, 1983–1994. Editor, *The Architects' Journal*, 1994–1999. Editor, *The Architectural Review*, 2005–2009. A commissioner at CABE, and Deputy Chair, 1999–2005. Chair, 2009–2011. Olympic Design Review Chair 2006–2010. Co-editor, *Planning in London* since 1992. Honorary FRIBA 1994; honorary member, Royal Society of Architects in Wales; honorary doctorate, University of Westminster, 2004; honorary fellowship, University College London, 2006; honorary member, British Council for Offices, 2006; honorary fellow, Royal Incorporation of Architects in Scotland, 2012. OBE for services to architecture, 2002.

MAX FORDHAM OBE, RDI, FRENG, HON FRIBA, PPCIBSE.

In 1966 Max founded the practice that evolved as Max Fordham LLP. The practice has aimed to bring an understanding of design to Environmental Engineering for buildings and architecture. For over 50 years Max has led the practice towards this aim. He is still a member of the practice but it now runs under its own democratic control and has a reputation for design through the strength of its engineering members, and their work. Max's contribution has been noted by many Honours and awards, but he is mostly known for environmental designs in various buildings, many of which have won Civic Trust Awards for their architecture and the sustainability of their design.

LEE MALLETT

Lee Mallett is co-Publisher / Editor of *Planning in London* magazine, and owns and publishes *Westminster Planning* and *City Planning* newsletters. He is former Editor of *Building Design* and *Estates Times* (now *Property Week*). His company URBIK helps developers, architects and regeneration agencies with their marketing, bids and communication needs. He was co-Chair of My City Too, an Open City campaign to improve urban design for young people. He was design advisor to Channel 4's 2008 TV series about regenerating the town of Castleford, *The Big Town Plan*. He is a steering committee member of the London Festival of Architecture. He has been a commentator on built environment issues since the mid-80s. He is a chartered surveyor.

SELINA MASON. MSC, DIP ARCH (CANTAB), ARB

Selina Mason joined the London Legacy Development Corporation (formerly the Olympic Park Legacy Company) in June 2011 as a secondee from the Olympic Delivery Authority. Her role there is to lead on the design of the post-Games Transformation of the park in advance of opening to the public in summer 2013. Selina joined the ODA in June 2007 as the ODA's Deputy Head of Design. Her role at the ODA was Project Sponsor for post-Games Transformation preparing and leading the design and delivery of the post-Games Transformation works. Her work at the ODA also covered design integration leadership, ensuring that the venues, facilities, and landscape delivered for the London 2012 Olympic and Paralympic Games and the legacy beyond created a coherent place of consistent high quality. Prior to joining the ODA, Selina was the Director of Design Review and Architecture at the Commission for Architecture and the Built Environment (CABE), a high profile role at the heart of some of the most significant planning decisions in England. She became a Director at CABE in 2005, having joined CABE in 2001 as a member of the Enabling team working with public sector clients, departments and agencies in a range of investment programmes including the Housing Market Renewal and Growth Areas. Selina is a qualified architect who has worked on a range of significant projects for both the public and private sectors, including the Falmouth Maritime Museum with Long & Kentish Architects. Before joining CABE in 2001 Selina completed a Masters in Urban and Regional Planning at London School of Economics.

C R E D I T S

COVER	DMA	23 Right	DG
		25	DG
FOREWORD	DMA	26 Left	MCC
		26 Right	DG
EVOLUTION VS REVOLUTION		27 Left	DG
8 / 9	TS	27 Top R	DMA
10	DMA	27 Bottom R	DMA
12	TS	28 Left	U
13	DMA	28 Right	P+M
14 Left	DG	29 Top	DMA
14 Right	DMA	29 Bottom	U
15 Left	JL	30	U
15 Right	JL	31 Left	DMA
16 Left	NB	31 Right	DMA
16 Right	CP		
18 Left	DMA	**NATURAL CONSEQUENCES**	
18 Right	MVS	32 / 33	C+M
19 Left	MVS	34	DMA
19 Right	MVS	36	DMA
21 Top	JM	37 Left	DMA
21 Bottom L	JM	37 Right	DMA
21 Bottom R	JM	38 Top L	DMA
22	DG	38 Bottom L	DMA
23 Left	DG	38 Right	DMA

Ref	Credit	Ref	Credit	Ref	Credit	Ref	Credit	Ref	Credit
39	SC	55 Bottom R	DMA	76 L–R	DMA	91 Left	P+M	108	DMA
40	SC	56	MH	76 L–R	DG	91 Top R	P+M	109	DMA
42 Left	MVS	57 Left	DMA	76 L–R	DA	91 Middle R	P+M		
42 Right	DMA	57 Right	DMA	76 L–R	DG	91 Bottom R	DMA	**TUNING IN**	
43	MVS	60 Top	DMA	76 L–R	U	92 Left	U	110 / 111	DMA
44 Top	MVS	60 Bottom	DMA	76 L–R	DG	92 Top R	DMA	112	DMA
44 Bottom	MVS	61	MH	76 L–R	JL	92 Bottom R	P+M	114	DMA
46	MVS	62	DMA	76 L–R	MVS	93	US	115	DMA
47 Left	DG	63	DMA	76 L–R	DG	94	DG	116 Left	DMA
47 Right	DG	65	DMA	76 L–R	RD	95	DMA	116 Right	DMA
48	DG	66	DMA	77 Left	DMA	96	DG	117 Left	MVS
49	DMA	67	DMA	77 Right	DMA	97 Left	DMA	118 Left	MVS
50 Top	DG	68 Top	DMA	79	DMA	98	DA	118 Right	MVS
50 Bottom	DG	68 Bottom	DMA	80	DG	100	DA	119 Left	DMA
51	DG	69 Top	DMA	81 Top	DMA	102	DMA	119 Right	DMA
52 Left	DMA	69 Bottom	DMA	82 Bottom	DG	103	DA	120	MVS
52 Right	DG	70	DMA	82	DMA	104 Top L	DA	121	MVS
53 Left	DG	71	DMA	83	DMA	104 Top R	DMA	122 Left	DMA
53 Right	DG			84	DMA	104 Bottom	DA / DMA	122 Right	A+M
54 Top L	DMA	**5-D GEOMETRY**		85	DMA	105	DMA	123 Top	MVS
54 Bottom L	B	72 / 73	DMA	86	DMA	106 Left	DMA	124	MVS
54 Right	DMA	74	DG	87	DMA	106 Right	DMA	125 Right	MVS
55 Left	DMA	76 L-R	DG	88	TS	107 Left	DMA	126 Left	DMA
55 Top R	DMA	76 L–R	DMA	89	DMA	107 Right	DMA	126 Right	MVS

127 Left	DMA	140	CH	158 Top	DMA	**DA**—Diane Auckland, Fotohaus Ltd
127 Right	DMA	141	CH	158 Bottom	DMA	**TS**—Tim Smith
128 Top R	DMA	142	DMA	159 Left	DG	**JL**—John Linden
128 Bottom R	DMA	143	DMA	159 Right	DMA	**NB**—Nic Bailey
129 Top	DMA			160	DMA	**CP**—Centre Pompidou—MnamCci—
129 Bottom	DMA	**INTEGRATION**		161 Top	JOS	Kandinsky Library—Maison du Peuple,
130 Left	DMA	144 / 145	MVS	161 Bottom	JOS	Clichy, 1935–1939. Centre Pompidou,
130 Right	DMA	146	DMA	162 Left	MVS	Paris, Bibliothéque Kandinsky, Fonds
131 Top	RD	148	DMA	162 Right	MVS	Jean Prouvé. © VG Bildkunst, Bonn
131 Bottom	DG	149	DMA	163 Left	MVS	**MVS**—Morley Von Sternberg
132 Left	DG	150 Top L	MVS	163 Right	DMA	**JM**—Jonathan Moore
132 Top R	DG	150 Bottom L	MVS	164 Top	DMA	**DG**—Dennis Gilbert
132 Bottom R	DG	150 Right	MVS	164 Bottom	DMA	**MCC**—Marylebone Cricket Club
133	DMA	151 Left	MVS	165	DG	**U**—Uniform
134 Left	DG	151 Right	MVS	166 Left	DMA	**C+M**—Colvin and Moggridge
134 Top	DG	152	DMA	166 Right	DMA	**SC**—Simon Collins
134 Bottom	DG	154 Bottom L	DG	168 Top	DMA	**B**—Biotecture
135	DG	154 Bottom R	TCC	168 Bottom	DMA	**MH**—Martin Hartley
136	JL	155 Left	DG	169	DMA	**P+M**—Price and Myers
137 Left	DMA	155 Right	DG			**US**—Urban Splash
137 Right	DMA	156 Left	DG	All line drawings	DMA	**A+M**—Allies and Morrison and Porphyrios
138	DMA	156 Right	RF			Architects with Townshends Landscape
139 Left	CH	157 Left	DG			Architects
139 Right	SH	157 Right	DG			**RD**—Richard Davis
						CH—Chris Hill
						SH—Steffan Hill
						RF—Professor Richard Frewer
						TCC—Talacre Community Sports Centre
						JOS—John Ogle-Skan courtesy of Galliford Try

T H A N K S

David Morley Architects operate a horizontal management structure which acknowledges that each project should be credited to a broad team of designers and support staff within the practice. Particular credit is due to the partners and associates who have helped to support and manage that wider team. After establishing the practice in 1987 David Morley formed a partnership with Jonathan Wilson in 1993. Andy Mytom and Ruth Butler joined the partnership in 2004 under the banner of David Morley Architects Limited Liability Partnership. Past associates included Alan Jones, Clive Gray, David Lewis, Gavin Pearce and Radhika Ponniah. In 2012 the management team benefit from the dedication and creativity of associates Mark Davies, Juliet Erridge, Helen James, David Preece and Chris Roberts, supported by partners David Morley and Andy Mytom.

The project summary sheets list out the team of other consultants and contractors who have been involved with the projects featured in this book and of course all the clients, who have had a special significance in facilitating David Morley Architects' portfolio.

In the making of *Five by 5*, special credit should go to Tessa Ball who, in addition to assembling much of the content, invented the name of the book. For the drawings, special thanks go to Despoina Kapodistria under the watchful eye of David Preece. Finally, much credit is due to Duncan McCorquodale and his team for their perseverance in designing and producing *Five by 5*.

COLOPHON

Copyright 2012 Artifice books on architecture, the authors and architects.
All rights reserved.

Artifice books on architecture
10a Acton Street
London WC1X 9NG
United Kingdom

Tel: +44 (0)20 7713 5097
Fax: +44 (0)20 7713 8682
sales@artificebooksonline.com
www.artificebooksonline.com

No part of this publication may be reproduced, stored in a retrieval system, or transmitted, in any form or by any means, electronic, mechanical, photocopying, recording, or otherwise, without prior permission of the publisher.

All opinions expressed within this publication are those of the authors and not necessarily of the publisher.

British Library Cataloguing-in-Publication Data A CIP record for this book is available from the British Library.

ISBN 978 1 907317 77 4

Artifice books on architecture is an environmentally responsible company. *Five by 5* is printed using sustainably sourced materials.

Designed at Artifice books on architecture
by Alex Prior with the assistance of Elin Svensson.